PARAPSYCHOLOGY
FROM DUKE TO FRNM
by J. B. Rhine and Associates

The Parapsychology Press
Durham, North Carolina

Preface

On July 30, 1964, a full day of celebration was held at Duke University in recognition of the establishment in Durham, North Carolina, two years earlier, of the Foundation for Research on the Nature of Man. This was the first Foundation Day of this new institution and it was projected as initiating the dedication of an annual day having this character and purpose.

For those who were unable to attend the meetings, the full schedule of activities on Foundation Day of 1964 is reproduced in the Appendix. It will be seen there that the main emphasis was on scientific papers. The forenoon session was devoted to the reading of a series of four papers reviewing the thirty-seven years of work at Duke, the period during which parapsychology emerged as a science.

The afternoon session was given to a series of six short reports of Duke researches in parapsychology current at the time, the selection affording a cursory "look through the window" of the Laboratory at the types of work and workers caught in transient focus. The evening session scheduled a paper on the state of parapsychology today.

This book is made up largely of these papers and the

comments with which they were introduced. The material is self-explanatory, and the comments were intended to provide the reader, like the audience, with introductory orientation. The publication of this volume is an attempt to extend to others who were not present an opportunity to share to some extent in the Foundation Day program.

A point remains that needs some clarification. Members of the audience to whom the material contained herein was first read were already acquainted with the aims and purposes of the Foundation, which was the focus of attention throughout the day. By way of the first *FRNM Bulletin,* which announced the formation of that organization, they had been given the reasons for the establishment of the Foundation, a statement of the co-operative arrangement with Duke University, an announcement of the plan for the Institute for Parapsychology as the first research unit, the election of a governing board, the appointment of an initial staff, and finally the setting-up of a financial goal. This introduction is needed by the reader as well; and for the convenience of those who have not seen the Announcement Bulletin of the FRNM, it, too, is reproduced in the Appendix.

Once this picture of the FRNM is in mind, the reasons for setting up the Foundation Day program as it was in 1964 can be more readily seen. With this background, something of the magnitude and vision of this venturesome undertaking will be appreciated, and the restraining of exaggerated optimism better understood. It will be clear that even with the measured step-by-step plan of advance which is outlined—a plan that concentrates solely at first upon the Institute of Parapsychology—the recognized need for a reserved and judicious appraisal of capability and a cautious program of commitment for the Foundation is a realistic one.

The FRNM may seem an ambitious conception, but hardly an impulsive or a visionary one. Rather, the background of past progress and achievement as represented by the history of parapsychology at Duke can itself provide considerable assurance on the side of future progress. Some further indication of capability may also be seen in the section of afternoon papers, representing personnel who are undergoing training for research in the parapsychological field. Finally, the sober, objective estimate of parapsychology at the present juncture given in the evening address should help to gauge the magnitude of the job ahead and the prospect for the success of the venture.

There is much, of course, of what the Foundation Day proceedings accomplished that cannot be expected to be found in these pages. The most notable effect, perhaps, is the vigorous group spirit spontaneously generated by the meetings. It seems most probable that such advanced confidence and heightened resolution as resulted could in themselves be determining, if not decisive, factors in the growth and accomplishment of the FRNM.

It was manifest above all that, however incompletely representative the group assembled may have been, it was at least a strongly united and a harmoniously dedicated company of explorers, ready to work together in the search for the knowledge which, they devotedly agreed, men need above all else to obtain. These pages will not, then, bring any indication of this recharging of morale that took place among many of those who participated in the July 30 convention. But they may, if read against the background of an appreciation of the vision of what the FRNM is intended to become, take on a value far beyond their own intrinsic worth. It might almost be said that it was the day that gave special significance to the papers, more than the papers that made the day.

J. B. R.

Parapsychology Laboratory
College Station, Durham, North Carolina

Contents

Part I

Parapsychology at Duke
1927-1965

The chapters in this section were written by Dr. J. B. Rhine. Except for the Introductory and Closing Remarks, however, they were read at the Foundation Day ceremonies by members of the staff of the Parapsychology Laboratory.

1

Introductory Remarks

by DR. J. B. RHINE, Chairman

On this first official Foundation Day, held to celebrate the establishment of the Foundation for Research on the Nature of Man, it would seem a proper beginning to turn for an appraising look backward across the years of parapsychology at Duke and to evaluate their contribution. To do so is especially appropriate now because this contribution is a necessary background for the larger forward action we are contemplating today.

There is another reason, also, to judge the progress of these former years with all possible wisdom and understanding. That reason is that we can, I think, find within the progress they represent the most reliable index of our capability for the future.

However, we have assembled here today for more than celebration. We hope also to draw from our conjoined resolution and ingenuity some of the added force we need for a confident stride into a very bold endeavor. To face, as we are doing, a steep and frontal assault upon the vast territory of man's unknown nature can rightly constitute a sobering and humbling experience. And even on such an occasion of candid congratulation and acknowledgment as this day is meant to be, this frank humility would seem entirely proper.

But the strength of forward thrust which the launching of our program will require can better be supplied, as we are all aware, by turning to observe the undeniable gains from the records of the past. Some of the needed confidence is thus supplied by the irreducible facts of hard-earned progress —progress made when the roads were even rougher than they are today—and accomplished with less encouragement because the scroll of achievement was shorter than that which we now present.

In the preparation of the papers to follow, we have reminded ourselves that the valid and enduring lift which history gives to the human spirit depends upon its independent truthfulness. It cannot carry the load we need to give it in this instance without a balanced objectivity which can be appreciated by fair and scholarly minds. While this is necessarily a story about a part of Duke University, it is not written as "a Duke development"; nor is it presented as a personal history, nor as an American or a Western presentation; rather, it is offered as a part of man's progressive scientific search for an understanding of the marks of his own identification.

These accounts have been submitted to many judgments for the acquisition of perspective and balance. As would be true of the content of its pages, this history would be wearying if its detailed acknowledgments required spelling out. But factual matter wears no better for explicit by-lining; and so this chronicle of the work of a modest laboratory, existing for a few decades in the middle of the twentieth century, in a new university, in a southern town, is now presented in four short chapters, each of them read by one whose contributions are themselves a part of the story—a chronicle presented for what it may be worth in those ultimate net values that are independent of locations and languages, of cultures and of times.

2

Beginnings in the Department of Psychology: ESP Established[1]

Parapsychology began at Duke with the Department of Psychology. Psychology was set up as a separate department with the arrival of Professor William McDougall, F.R.S., the distinguished British psychologist who had been brought from Harvard in the fall of 1927 by the founding president of the University, Dr. William Preston Few. It was in September of that same year that two young biologists, Dr. J. B. Rhine and his wife, Dr. Louisa E. Rhine, came to Duke for a period of post-doctoral study, under Professor McDougall, of the claims to scientific value of the field known as psychical research.

The reason for the coming of the Rhines to Duke was the fact that Professor McDougall was the man best prepared at that time to serve as a mentor in the difficult appraisal they had come to make. Along with his distinction as a psychologist of especially broad experience and training, he had given

1. Delivered by Dr. Winnifred Nielsen.

a considerable share of his attention to the problems of psychical research as well.

The special mission which brought the Rhines to Duke, although it did not measure the entire range of their interest in psychical matters, had to do with the claims of mediumistic communication with discarnate personalities, the question of spirit survival. Even more specifically, they had come laden with a large collection of records of stenographic notes taken at sittings with mediums, with the aim of evaluating this material under the guidance of Professor McDougall. This material belonged to the Assistant Superintendent of Schools of the city of Detroit, Mr. John F. Thomas, and it was with his financial support that their visit to Duke was made.

It is of some importance to note that parapsychology came to Duke because of an interest in the problem of post-mortem survival, not only on the part of the sponsor, Mr. Thomas, but on the part of the Rhines and Dr. McDougall as well. In fact, so tolerant on the question was the new Department of Psychology, and also the Duke administration itself, that after a few years Mr. Thomas was granted the Ph.D. degree for a thesis based upon the studies made at Duke on his mediumistic records. Incidentally, this doctorate, given in 1932, was the first one to be granted for a thesis in parapsychology in an American university.

Two important points deserve special discussion in connection with this beginning at Duke: first, the fact that it was possible for such a beginning to be made at that university; and second, that the primary emphasis of the research and the thesis was on the topic of post-mortem survival. It is very doubtful if parapsychology could have made a comparable beginning in the department of psychology at any other American university in 1927. (For that matter, nothing comparable has occurred since that time, in spite of the example at Duke.) Among the numerous advantages at Duke was the fact that the University had just been established a few years earlier. The founding president, Dr. Few, was in the process of building a staff; and with the opening of a new department of psychology, the only one whose approval was needed for attention to parapsychology was the Chairman of the Department, Professor McDougall, who was deeply interested in the field to begin with. The President of the University was himself personally interested in the investigations in parapsychology. Then, too, at that stage, the growth of organization that leads to a more conventional regulation of the intellectual life of a university community was only beginning. Duke was, accordingly, the one place where, and the late 1920's perhaps the one time when, the implantation of a healthy beginning of a research program in parapsychology could have been brought about.

The second point is the emphasis given to the studies of mediumship and possible communication with incorporeal ("spirit") personalities. This will seem more unusual today to the student of parapsychology than it appeared in 1927. It is important, however, to realize that it was this same "survival" problem that brought parapsychology to scientific attention anywhere. There had, of course, been scattered instances of attention given to other parapsychical claims (for example, in connection with mesmerism or hypnotism), but it was the Spiritualist movement more than anything else that drew scientific interest to the associated claims. As always in the vanguard of scientific progress, here was a strong and widespread human need—in this case, the need to know whether any continuation of personality beyond the grave could be demonstrated.

Long before the investigations began at Duke, inquirers in the psychical research societies had recognized that communication with discarnate minds would be a sort of telepathy, and this reflection made that alleged phenomenon a problem for scientific investigation. The further possibility that telepathy between the medium and the living might account for the communication of knowledge the medium could not have gained sensorially added further grounds for taking the investigation of telepathy seriously. Also, besides telepathy, other related powers were bracketed in the classification of psychical phenomena, the field of psychical research.

So it may be seen that at the time parapsychology came to Duke, the field, as is shown by the contents of the journals and proceedings of the psychical research societies of the time, was dominated by the investigations of spirit communication through mediumship. Other psychical phenomena had not as yet received sufficient independent support and interest to have led the way in such a development. Most of the financial support for work in psychical research up to that time (and for long after) came from persons primarily interested in the survival problem. Most of the leading inquirers in psychical research at the time, like the Rhines, were led to their interest through the challenging problem of the occurrence of post-mortem communication.

It should be added that in that day the depth of interest of eminent scholars in claims of proof of spirit survival easily surpassed anything comparable in the current situation in parapsychology today. At that time the significance of the problem for human destiny was obvious—to say nothing of its psychological and biological implications—provided it could be taken seriously by science. The Spiritualists had made a faith out of the claims of spirit survival and communication and thus had brought attention to the phenomena of mediumship and related manifestations. The work begun at Duke was designed to pursue the question with all the facilities the psychology laboratory offered and to bring to the research the full advantages of the community of university scholarship. In the light of this background, the program of the Department of Psychology in sponsoring the thesis on mediumship by Mr. Thomas, and other developments that will be mentioned later, can be somewhat better understood.

Almost immediately, however, the studies of the Thomas records of mediumistic utterances brought sharply into focus the question of the true source of the information given by the medium. Taking the annotated records at face value for a tentative judgment, it soon appeared that the information given by the various mediums with whom Mr. Thomas had worked by the use of token sittings (that is, when the sitter was represented only by a stenographer and a token object) was explainable only by the hypothesis that some source of information from beyond the medium herself was involved. How the medium could get this information from another person, living or dead, was not known, but at least the possibility of getting it extrasensorially from the living could be investigated. Experiments had already been conducted to test the claims of thought transference or telepathy, and a few on clairvoyance as well. But few scholarly people had thought of the evidence given in these tests as adequate for conclusions. J. B. Rhine, who, after his first year, was on the staff of the Department of Psychology, undertook to experiment with telepathy and clairvoyance and was joined for a time by other colleagues on the Department staff. Students also took part in the investigations, and a number of them became active as workers in the field of parapsychology on their own in later years. A particularly wholesome cooperative relationship developed on all levels of activity, and, under Professor McDougall's leadership, a spirit of departmental unity on the psychical research project prevailed. This was especially important in the development of methods and standards on which critical judgment from different points of view is important.

As tests of telepathy and clairvoyance were undertaken, the first procedures were those which had been developed in the initial work in the field as it had been done in other lands and times. This was as it should be. While the results obtained at first were barely encouraging enough to warrant continuing, they sufficed to bring out the need for better, more orderly testing techniques. With students volunteering as test subjects, it was necessary to do short, lively test series that would encourage in the individual an interest in his performance and a desire to come back for more tests. This was a fortunate circumstance because it was later found that the subject's interest is an important condition for the successful demonstration of ESP.

A special set of test cards was developed, and this has now become a more-or-less standard item of equipment in any laboratory of parapsychology, although it has since gone through many adaptations and modifications. The basic test procedure for clairvoyance was a simple matter of guessing cards under conditions that insured, first, that sensory cues were rendered impossible, and, second, that a mathematical appraisal of the results could be properly made. With the help of the Duke Department of Mathematics and other mathematicians elsewhere, it was found possible to apply standard techniques to estimate the extrachance significance of the results obtained. Then, with the help of subjects selected on the basis of past work, test after test could be carried out with progressive improvement of safeguards, such as increasing the distance between the subject and the cards he tried to identify, so that eventually there seemed to be no reasonable alternative to the hypothesis that some kind of extrasensory perception was responsible for the results obtained.

The climax of the clairvoyance tests was reached in the fall of 1933, when, with an outstanding and well-tested subject (H. P.), J. B. Rhine and a student assistant, J. G. Pratt, carried out a series of tests of the clairvoyant type of ESP, in which considerable distance was involved. The subject (H. P.) was located in a building at least 100 yards from the room in which the test cards were placed. The experimental assistant handled the cards at the rate of one per minute without seeing the faces, while the subject attempted to identify them. The two men kept time with synchronized watches, recorded the cards and responses in duplicate, and as an added precaution, turned over the duplicate copies to Dr. Rhine at the end of the session.

When, after a specified series of 300 trials, H. P. obtained a total score of approximately twice the number of hits expected from "chance" and it was found that this result represented odds against chance of a fantastically large figure, it was decided to publish a report of the work with the conclusion that the securing of information without the use of the senses had been demonstrated. In a monograph, *Extra-Sensory Perception,*[2] published by the Boston Society for Psychical Research in 1934 that work and that conclusion were published.

Even as the manuscript went to the printer, the experiments with H.P. were continuing with the aim of ever-increasingly stringent precautions against sensory cues, one of the subsequent series following a procedure in which *both* Dr. Rhine and Mr. Pratt were present throughout the session to guard against error and insure the conduct of the experiment as designed. Results under these conditions confirmed the already conclusive case, and, after the manner of scientific research, the matter was presented as a monograph for criticism and for possible repetition by other experimenters.

The monograph contained other contributions beyond the development of the case for the clairvoyant type of extra-sensory perception; for example, it was realized in the Duke work that the experimental methods used in all the previous tests of telepathy had not really provided a test of telepathy at all. There had always been a person acting as a sender or agent who looked at the object, the image of which was to be transferred telepathically. This condition, of course, would equally well allow the possibility that the subject whose

2. Reprinted in paperback in 1964 by Bruce Humphries, Boston.

ability was being tested might be using clairvoyance rather than telepathy if he obtained results that were better than those to be expected from chance. It turned out, then, that the first experiment on record which could actually test telepathy was one carried out in the Duke Laboratory after a method had been designed whereby the sender would have no objective target or record available at the time the trial was made. In this way, tests that were called "pure telepathy" were carried out and compared with results obtained in clairvoyance tests in which telepathy was excluded. Comparable scoring rates were produced on the two types of tests, and the exploratory work of this period led to the conclusion that extrasensory perception might be either clairvoyant or telepathic in type, although later on, questions about the adequacy of these techniques themselves were raised and further work was needed.

While a range of other exploratory experiments was presented in the monograph and the doors were opened upon many important research problems, the one definitely conclusive point made was the apparently firm establishment of the clairvoyant type of ESP. The establishment of clairvoyance and the development of standard test procedures for further investigations represented the chief contribution of the period. The subject of parapsychology had been opened up for scientific exploration.

The monograph in 1934, mentioned above, was not received with public indifference. Instead of the findings being generally ignored as some indications had led the Duke workers to expect they might be, a somewhat explosive reaction resulted. Although the book was published obscurely and was written with no attempt at popular appeal, it was picked up by the Science Editor of the *New York Times*, Waldemar Kaempffert, who gave it a strongly favorable review. Other attention followed, until many of the national magazines had published articles on the new investigations in extrasensory perception. A radio broadcast on a national network dealing with popular discussions and tests identified with ESP ran for nine months.

Some explanation of this wide popular interest is in order since it had a very important effect upon the progress of parapsychology. The movement for the popularization of science was still at that time a new and growing one. Science writers over the country were almost to a man eagerly looking for new and interesting science which the public could understand, and with one exception, they gave the research on ESP a fair and ample coverage. There were, it is true, some unavoidable excesses by other writers and broadcasters, but for the most part the publicity was suitably educational.

Realizing that this wave of public interest would have a disturbing effect upon colleagues and professional psychologists in general, Dr. Rhine instituted a conservative policy toward the release of news, allowing only published work to be reported on. For a number of years he permitted no releases to go out from the Office of Public Information of the University because this would give the appearance of promotion. Today, with a longer, calmer look, it can be seen that there was a ready, natural interest on the part of the intelligent public and a recognition that something was being done at Duke that had long needed to be done, something which brought the light of scientific clarification into an area that had been left too long to less scholarly methods of treatment. What then appeared to be a sensational and temporary wave of interest has developed into a steady and continuing flow. There has been no cessation over the years. The public is waiting still today with a better prepared expectation and a more serious and cautious judgment for each new advance parapsychology has to offer. But it was in the years following the first publication that workers in parapsychology came to realize that a genuine public interest was on their side.

Promotion and salesmanship were not needed. The desire for knowledge was, and is, there; and it is very general.

But the effect of this flare-up of publicity over the Duke experiments in ESP was by no means wholly beneficial to parapsychology. It is true, it did lead to much encouragement, both from the Duke administration, which was appreciative of public interest in the University, and from newly made friends who made it possible through grants of financial aid to acquire the help of several student assistants. These were important advantages, but far outweighing them was the surprising vigor of the hostile reaction of a number of psychologists. They were undoubtedly shocked by the sensational publicity over these revolutionary findings. They could not know that all the public excitement was as much a surprise to the Duke workers as it was to them and that the publicity was a product of public interest in the findings, not of any promotion given to publicizing them.

As a consequence, a few men who would have felt only a tolerant pity for the parapsychologist, venturing so far out of the range of orthodoxy, boiled up for a time in a towering rage of denunciation of the national craze they thought must have been deliberately generated and whipped up by irresponsible sensationalism. It was an atmosphere so acrid and clouded by the smoke of dissension as not to permit a calm judgment of the real merits of the findings presented. Criticisms were overdone, phrased in intemperate language, and published far too easily and incautiously.

During this period of tension, the Duke administration was subjected to strong pressures, both private and public; but there was never a sign of vacillation throughout the entire controversy. President Few himself introduced J. B. Rhine in a public lecture to a full house in Page Auditorium in 1936, staunchly vouched for the soundness of the research, and made reference to his own personal experiences of extrasensory character. His successor, Dr. Robert Lee Flowers, in giving Dr. Rhine the franchise to continue the investigations under his administration, testified from his personal observation to the confidence he had in the importance of the program.

But the appearance of the first book and the reaction that followed marked more than the drawing of the issue with the scientific world. Naturally, perhaps inevitably, it created a departmental situation as well. The account of this belongs in the chapter that follows.

3

Parapsychology Becomes a Branch of Science[3]

The divisions of history, like those of geography, tend to follow natural features. The preceding chapter ended with the dividing line of critical reaction to the first report of the ESP work at Duke, a line that marked a sharp issue between the new results and the recognized areas of knowledge.

This dividing line was, of course, an external matter. But there was also one that arose within the Department of Psychology itself, a unit that by 1934 consisted of five members, including Professor McDougall as Chairman.

Up until the publication of the monograph and for a short time thereafter, during which there was no indication of public reaction to it, the departmental staff had been a harmonious group. All were unusually united under the leadership of their respected chief. When, however, public attention was turned rather strongly upon the investigations of

3. Delivered by Dr. John A. Freeman.

ESP, a noticeable change of internal atmosphere began to manifest itself. As publicity mounted, funds became available for this particular branch of the Department's research, and signs of administrative appreciation of the public interest were to some extent evident. From this time on, more or less incidental indications were given of an effect of this public interest upon some of the other members. It should be added, however, that such effects would probably have occurred in any other academic department and in any university.

At this point, Dr. Rhine requested the Department and the University for permission to give the work he supervised a distinctive name and organization. With the approval of Professor McDougall, he selected the word "parapsychology" as a translation of the German word "parapsychologie," and the designation for the psychical research section of the Department of Psychology became known as the Parapsychology Laboratory. Along with this transition in 1935 came also the establishment of a special fund named the William McDougall Research Fund, set up to help finance the special needs of the Parapsychology Laboratory.

From the perspective of later analysis the move to give parapsychology its own designation appears to have been a wise and helpful one. This judgment can be made without undue reflection upon the attitudes of any of those concerned. A very real problem was created by the growth of the research in parapsychology and its appeal to the general public, one that could have seriously affected the morale of the departmental staff. This step toward adjustment afforded relief, relief that was partly due to the effort of attempting to find a solution.

The studies in parapsychology at Duke had begun, however, as part of the program of psychology. Professor McDougall thought of them that way, and so had most of the others who had attempted to classify the problems of psychical research. But there can be no doubt that the formation of the Parapsychology Laboratory and the designation of the branch of studies concerned as "parapsychology" was the initial recognition of a real division between psychology proper and parapsychology, one that has become more evident since then. As will later be seen, we now realize that parapsychology cannot be accommodated within the presently conceived field of general psychology; it could be added on to or merged with, but not included by, the general field. However, this was not apparent to anyone in 1935. The separation made at that time was purely a matter of convenience and good relations. There was much talk, then even, about the temporary character of the prefix "para"; but there has been little mention of it in recent years.

What would have happened had the public reacted with indifference to the publication of *Extra-Sensory Perception* in 1934? It seems probable that no serious problems in the Department would ever have arisen. It would likely have been the same had the investigation been pursued with no more than the usual vigor of faculty research. The well-known situation at Stanford University might illustrate the consequence that would most probably have followed. Psychical research would easily have become buried and forgotten.

In the new Parapsychology Laboratory, primary attention was already shifting to the development of a wide range of test procedures, but there was still a large preoccupation with the original problem of post-mortem communication. A somewhat climactic development in the study of mediumship in fact occurred right in the midst of the changes in organization already described.

While parapsychology was still a part of the undivided department, an offer was made to Professor McDougall by a well-known British medium, Mrs. Eileen J. Garrett, to contribute her time and services for a scientific study of the trance phenomena of her mediumship. The offer was unanimously accepted and Dr. Rhine was given charge of the investigation. With the assistance of a number of graduate students (among them J. G. Pratt and C. E. Stuart), a series of experimental sittings were held under conditions of control considerably more guarded than had ever been used before in mediumistic studies. By the use of two rooms, all sensory knowledge of the sitter was kept from the medium; and at the same time, it was possible to obtain an objective or blind annotation of the sitting records by each of the sitters. From the best possible statistical analysis of the results available at that time, it seemed clear that the medium had obtained, from some source, information that was relevant to the sitters for whom it was given. It was a distinctive step forward to be able to conclude this under the strict evaluative methods that were used.

But even while these trance experiments were going on, parallel tests of the medium's ESP ability were made, in both the waking and the trance state, for telepathy and for clairvoyance. It was clear from the results of these tests that she possessed abilities which would have enabled her to acquire from sources in the environment and the living world the information she produced in her mediumistic messages. There was no need to attribute the results in the one case to discarnate agencies any more than there was in the other. This research, accordingly, for the first time brought the method of studying mediums and the question of their validity into experimental focus.

It was now necessary to devise a new experimental approach if progress was to be made toward the solution of the problem of post-mortem survival. Here on the one hand was the soundest evidence yet that a medium could acquire information by extrasensory means; but here too, on the other hand, was evidence which offered an alternative explanation to that of incorporeal agency. And this can be added: that there the matter was left when the reports were published and even when, twenty-five years later, a symposium was held at Duke to reappraise the situation. There the matter still stands, as indicated by the series published in the *Journal of Parapsychology* in its volume for 1960.

It seemed all the more urgent, then, to push the program of research on extrasensory perception to find the extent of its reach as well as its limitations. This would be one of the ways to pursue the investigation of the stalemated question of survival itself. In any case, the very hypothesis of survival depended upon extrasensory perception, even for its mode of communication through mediums. To the workers at Duke, however, there was no lack of stimulus to pursue the investigation of the abilities for which the evidence had been accumulating for some years.

With the case for clairvoyant ESP rather firmly established and that for telepathy, too, according to the requirements at that stage, the interest of the research staff turned to other types of parapsychical phenomena, types suggested by spontaneous experiences and the conditions under which they occurred. It had already been indicated that distances over which the ESP experiments had been conducted did not seem to show any relation to the results obtained. Not only in spontaneous experiences had there been ample indication of a complete independence of distance, but even in experiments such as described with H.P. in the preceding chapter a distance of 100 yards or more allowed results of as high a scoring level as those in which the target was within a yard of the subject.

In the collections of spontaneous case material, too, there was a large section in which knowledge of future events was apparently received in much the same way as knowledge of distant events. If the cases were to be taken seriously, it appeared that precognitive ESP was occurring as frequently as other types. With this background it seemed logical enough to test the subjects who showed ESP ability for their capacity to direct it upon *future* target orders, and the card tests lent themselves to that modification.

Then began a long series of steps in the development of adequate tests of precognition, a development that lasted over many years. One by one, new methods were found to yield what looked like better evidence of precognition; later reflection, however, on the part of some member of the group found each of them inadequate on some point or other. The first test began with the prediction of the order of packs of cards as it would be after a certain limited period of hand-shuffling had taken place. This method allowed other possibilities besides precognition, and mechanical shuffling was introduced as the next improvement. Still later came the cutting of packs of cards by numbers derived from natural events, such as temperature readings on a specified date. We need not here pursue the matter all the way to the present stage; but it does seem that today, many years after the acceptance of the techniques now in use, the question of the occurrence of precognition has been answered in the affirmative.

As a matter of fact, the first known experiments on prophecy were carried out in the Duke Laboratory with the subject H.P. in December, 1933. These tests came about as just one of the many steps of experimental advance through which the studies have progressed. On the map of nature there was no boundary to cross. Space-time does not limit ESP and so there was no interference as a result of interposing either time or space barriers. To the scientist educated in today's schools, however, precognition must appear to be logically impossible. For this reason special care was taken to control the experiments against all alternative hypotheses. Understandably, it will be some time before the university that harbored the research which established the occurrence of precognition will know with confidence whether to feel proud or just a little embarrassed.

Another area of test development was running a close parallel with that of precognition throughout the period of this chapter. In early 1934 experimenters began tests of what has come to be called psychokinesis, or the direct action of mind over matter; that is, action without physical intermediation. Through human history there have been occasional reports of unusual physical happenings that suggested some sort of mental agency, either that of living individuals or of discarnate beings. Logically, too, the very parallel of ESP with sensory perception suggested another parallel between motor and extramotor response. The latter is better known as psychokinesis, or PK. And, finally, the analogy from the physical sciences of the law of reaction (for every action there is a reaction) suggested that in a subject's interaction with an object in ESP there might be some unknown reversible energetic principle.

The question of how such an idea could be tested was solved by the suggestion of using the familiar belief in the ability to influence dice in games. The dice-throwing operation needed only to be dressed up by technical refinements and subjected to good experimental design to afford a suitable laboratory test of PK. A decade of refinements and repetitions and a vast accumulation of test results from many observers were needed before the first publication was released in 1943. In the years that followed there was a long series of contributions to the evidence for psychokinesis. The really climactic development of the case for PK, however, consisted of the discovery of lawful patterns that persisted throughout the comparative analysis of many series of independently conducted tests. Distribution of hits on the record page (or in other recording units) shows a high degree of orderly relation to position on the page. Only the operation of PK could provide a reasonable explanation for these significant hit distributions. The strength of this kind of evidence lies in the fact that it is waiting for the inquiring mind for re-examination, like the strata of the earth for the geologist. Here is something objective, repeatable, conclusive.

The case for PK thus can also be added to the significant findings of the Parapsychology Laboratory at Duke. In this branch, however, even more than in the case for precognition and clairvoyance, there has been independent confirmation by other laboratories, and this has strengthened the conclusion very materially.

One by one, then, the four types of parapsychical phenomena (or *psi* phenomena, as Thouless and Wiesner in England proposed they be called) came to be established. The case for telepathy was for a number of reasons still the weakest of the four. The difficulty of fastening adequate controls upon two persons, a sender and a receiver, greatly complicated the problem of controlling the experimental technique. It is safe to say that the progress of parapsychology would have been very much slower if the Duke workers had not chosen to make their first investigations with clairvoyance tests rather than telepathy. It came to be the policy to use telepathy tests only when no other form of psi test would serve the purpose.

There was, of course, one type of research which definitely required a test of telepathy, and that was the question whether or not telepathy was a genuine occurrence. The earlier Duke experiments on telepathy had been conducted with the sender waiting until after the receiver had recorded his response before the target would be recorded. In this way, it was thought, the receiver's possible clairvoyant ability would not be able to make use of the record. When, however, precognition was sufficiently well enough established to be a reasonable explanatory factor, the proposal was made that in telepathy tests the receiver might be using precognitive clairvoyance to give him advance information on the target to be recorded after the trial. Thereafter, in order to make a really *pure* telepathy test, even this later recording of the target had to be eliminated. This requirement greatly complicated the test procedure, but it was possible to devise a test in which telepathy could be tested without this record, and even a recheck of the results by an independent investigator could be added to the safeguards. A team of workers at the Duke Laboratory finally negotiated this difficult operation, and it was later repeated in England. And thus telepathy was "repurified" once more.

Then there arose a comparable problem about clairvoyance: Could the results obtained in clairvoyance tests be alternatively explained by supposing the subject might be using precognitive telepathy as a means of discovering what was on the unseen card by merely *going ahead in time* until the experimenter was looking at the card? This question was dealt with sufficiently well at the time when it seemed to be a problem. However, there has been a growing tendency to think of ESP as one basic process of which the differentiation into telepathy, clairvoyance, and precognition is only superficial and phenomenological. It now seems clear that ESP is a unitary process and not three fundamentally different ones. It is easier, too, in considering the evidence of PK, to think of one basic psi function involving interaction between subject and object in some sort of energetic exchange that, like the whole relation between the subject and his environment, remains to be explored. This larger problem is not confined to parapsychology, though parapsychology may be the science that will first find a way of bridging the gap.

The intensive preoccupation with these types of psi carried the workers of the Laboratory past certain broad generalizations without much thought as to their significance at the time. The focus was on each specific type of phenomenon until all four were rounded up and finally corralled by adequately conclusive tests and sufficient confirmation. But the generalizations were there; and they, more than the individual phenomena, contribute to the making of a science. By the time a decade of the publication of *The Journal of Parapsychology* had passed and J. B. Rhine reviewed the record of the preceding decades in his *Reach of The Mind,* parapsychology began to look like a science. First, it had a field distinctively its own, uncontested by any neighboring science; the field had a definable boundary and a classifiable range of phenomena for the testing of which a methodology had been developed and proven through years of controversial exchange. Moreover, although the methodology and organization had emerged from the Duke Laboratory, the methods had been taken over in other parts of the country and in other countries, to the extent that no one center alone was responsible for the principal findings.

The methods of this new science were, in principle, the methods of natural science in general. The mathematics which were applied to the evaluation of the results were those in standard use. The canons of evidence and the logic of interpretation made no undue concessions and upheld the best traditions of the philosophy of science. Certain properties general to the phenomena of parapsychology were found and now have been sufficiently extended to justify the confidence that an adequate rationale is emerging. To this the following chapters will contribute.

It seems proper, then, to recognize that we have a body of information that can logically be grouped into the unitary organization which makes a science. To be sure, every science is recognizedly only a branch of the larger science of nature, and this is true of parapsychology. That it is also a part of a larger ideally conceived branch of psychology and of a larger biological section of the science of nature is beyond argument. The phenomena of parapsychology have to be a part of a universal energy system as well. Only so can the phenomena of the field be accounted for; or to put it the other way around, there has to be something within the universal energy system to account for psi phenomena, just as for any other type of phenomena. While we are proceeding to learn more about this psi energy, we can recognize even now that in order to be observed it has to be interactive with at least some of the energy states already recognized in the physical sciences. This idea of the interconvertibility of psi energy takes account of the fact that psi phenomena can be radically different from those on the physical level and still belong to the more inclusive energetic universe. This newly discovered energy accommodates as well to the order of nature as the now well-recognized types of energy seemed to do at a comparable stage. Of course large unknowns are still left for future research, just as is true in all other branches of science.

By assuming a specific energetic determinant of its own, then, the science of parapsychology has adapted its findings to the logic of causality characteristic of the physical sciences themselves. It becomes broadly identifiable with the older branches of natural science, with the exception of physics itself; and with this it integrates under the assumption that there is a universal energetic system to which the physical order of nature is subordinate. This is for the physical sciences a revolutionary development comparable to the effect of the psi research upon psychology.

Evidently, then, if parapsychology has become a science, it is a science for the limited group of those who are informed about it. It was evident from the first publication in 1934 that it was not soon to be recognized as a science by the profession of psychologists. Probably nothing in the history of psychology so vigorously challenged the prevailing conception of that field as did the claims regarding extrasensory perception in the mid-1930's. In fact, when the American Psychological Association, which met in Columbus, Ohio, in September, 1938, held a series of symposia to consider and debate the evidence for ESP, it was quite obviously a test of the very right of the ESP workers to continue their researches. The fact that the research staff returned to Duke with renewed confidence made it clear that the meeting was a victory for the new science. The critical attacks from that time on were few and were increasingly ineffectual. The attacks on the mathematics had, in any case, ceased after the favorable judgment released by the President of the Institute of Mathematical Statistics in December, 1937. The better experimental conditions were not subjected to attack after the Columbus meeting. The controversy was plainly on the wane.

Here and there, it is true, a special interest remained to activate criticism of the Duke research. One such interest had developed because of the existence of a large sum of money which had been left to a university in the far west for use in psychical research, and the natural feeling of many elsewhere that the university was obligated to use the money for the purpose intended. It seemed no accident that by far the two most bitter and most extensive attacks made upon the Duke investigations were supported by this western university—and by funds which had been given to it for the purpose of *advancing* such research.

Our terms, then, have to be qualified in saying that paraspychology is a science, or even for that matter in saying that the case for ESP is established. It has not been established for the western university just mentioned. The occurrence of ESP has not been established as yet to the satisfaction of more than a small minority of the academic psychologists of this country—at any rate, when the last survey was made in 1955. Much the same qualifications must be made correspondingly for the statement that parapsychology is now a science. It is certainly not considered a science by those who are unacquainted with its findings; and for most people the use of the word "science" carries with it the implication that the field is accepted by the other sciences.

We have, then, to concede that it is only in the idealized

conception of scientific truth that we may properly claim that parapsychology is a legitimate branch of science. The point that is most important on this question of the status of parapsychology is that over the years and from the standpoint of the world as a whole, the new science has been improving its status not only in regard to its findings and their reliability but on the point of recognition as well. Over the last decade new centers of research have been opened in this country and abroad. A few courses in parapsychology are being offered, a textbook was prepared at Duke, and here and there a professorship of parapsychology has been instituted. A society of professional workers in the field was started at Duke in 1957 and has grown steadily in numbers. These and other signs give the indications needed that there is progress in the field, slow as it may be; but for a science that is revolutionary not only for psychology but also for the basic materialistic philosophy that has dominated the entire world of science, recognition must be expected to be tardy. If, by the end of the first half of the century, it had become evident to the Duke workers themselves that they were dealing with a distinct branch of science that had a definite area of natural phenomena of its own to claim, it would not have occurred to any of them to anticipate a universal acceptance of the fact much before the end of the century.

4

The Place of Psi in the Natural Order[4]

The third section of the story of parapsychology at Duke departs from the simple chronological account. Since it will deal with a more advanced stage in the progress of the science, it needs to be presented with less of the definite timing of developments than the foregoing papers. It overlaps considerably with the preceding period, as it will in a similar way with the one that comes next.

But nonetheless, it will make a discernible unit of effort and accomplishment. It will deal with the discoveries that were made when the Duke researches turned away from merely attempting to verify the occurrence of psi ability, or one or another of its types of phenomena, to the next stage in logical scientific development. This is the stage of discovering the relation of the phenomena, as far as such relations exist, to the already recognized divisions of the natural sciences. The thoughts of every worker in parapsychology turned, almost from the beginning, to questions of how such new findings could be fitted in with the rest of nature. The facts about

4. Delivered by Dr. K. Ramakrishna Rao.

psi were being substantiated, and therefore there had to be some underlying natural principles to account for them. Since the accumulating results really did *not* harmonize with accepted natural science, the situation offered an ideal opportunity for the inquiring mind. There had to be some explanation, but it was one that still had to be found. This is still the challenge of psi today.

*   *   *   *   *   *

The first test of the nature of psi was bound to be a physical one. All other modes of communication are recognizably physical; but one of the ways in which spontaneous psi manifestations challenged natural law was that they appeared to take place, as a rule, under circumstances in which no conceivable physical explanation could be supposed. Thus they gave the appearance of magic or miracle; and it is easily understandable, therefore, that religious practice—and theory as well—could take for granted powers that can now be identified as parapsychical.

Fortunately, tests of the possible physical character of psi ability were among the most easy and convenient to carry out. As already noted in the first chapter, comparisons of distance were introduced in 1933. Distances of the order of hundreds of yards seemed not to make any difference in results, as of course was to be expected from the spontaneous case records. Later distance comparisons ran to thousands of miles, and while the kind of precise comparison and measurement that would be possible in the physical sciences was never reached, the effort to get such was not required and not to be expected at this exploratory stage. The research that had been accomplished was sufficient to reveal any gross relationship that might exist between ESP and distance and to interpose barriers of physical nature such as would have been expected to inhibit the effect if familiar modes of communication had been in operation. There the matter had to be left for that stage; the comparison of distance went far enough to justify the appropriate next step—the introduction of tests of precognition, the ESP of future events. These tests also were begun before the year 1933 had closed.

A mere paragraph cannot do justice to the many-sided and careful stone-turning search for possible physical conditions that might reveal a positive connection between psi success and objective conditions, for *some* kind of hidden relationship was more or less assumed. Whatever causality ultimately may come to mean, it is a way of thought difficult to escape in dealing with nature firsthand. It has been shown in the tests so far that in psi something effective happens between subject and object, no matter how great the distance involved. Likewise, in the thirty years of precognition experiments, the results have shown no relation to time differences as far as they have been tested, which is up to one year. A wealth of related experimental results supported the general conclusion that psi communication was not in itself conditioned by physical variations such as the range of target objects, the position of the object, and a screen between subject and object, to mention a few of the most obvious. And yet it did seem necessary to think that psi was an exchange between subject and object and that, therefore, some transfer took place, that a determining influence between them was exerted. For what it was worth, it seemed best to hold on to the concept of causality as long as it could make sense.

The line of thought vigorously pushed was naturally the supposition that an unknown energy must be involved, either some departure from those types of energy already known or something entirely new. The suggestion of running tests of the *known* energy range was dismissed, especially when the evidence for precognition began to come in. What was the use of putting subjects in electrically screened cages to exclude radiation when precognition, which requires the existence of no present target whatever, could be shown to occur?

Yet the problem of clinging to a causality rationale to explain psi communication was, at the same time, complicated by the evidence for precognition itself. For most workers in the field and even in the Laboratory at Duke, this impossibility of explanation only served to make the establishment of a satisfactory case for precognition more difficult; that is, it gave a certain added importance to any remotely conceivable alternative. But at the same time, it increased the importance of pursuing the precognition hypothesis beyond all boundaries of doubt. The pursuit is still, of course, an open one for those who feel that those boundaries have not even yet been passed to their satisfaction. But again, the precognitive case material, which has accumulated at the Laboratory to an impressive extent, has been supported by one experimental study after another as the years of work have continued; so that now this particularly difficult and challenging corner of the field—ESP of the future—has been well established. Because of this work alone the physical energies are ruled out.

On the other hand, the concept that an energetic operation is necessarily involved in psi phenomena has the same logical support it has in any other branch of nature. The psi tests have repeatedly shown quantitatively measurable effects that are not attributable to any of the physical energy ranges. It was for this "capacity to effect measurable results" that the concept of energy was originally invented by man. True. enough, the energy involved here is still an unknown one; but this only serves to bring attention to the fact that the science of parapsychology is far from complete.

The main point is that the concept of a psi energy makes sense in understanding how causal interaction between subject and object can occur between a person in a psi test and the target object. It makes a point for the study of what it is that makes psi work. The hypothetical new energy can now be studied as a problem in itself.

The interpretation, then, which the psi researchers at Duke would tend to give the aspect of man shown in psi ability requires that psi be fitted *on* rather than fitted *into* the conception of the universe prevalent in the sciences today. Something more than at present recognized is needed, not only in man but in the universe as a whole, to accommodate the findings of these Duke investigations and confirmatory ones in other laboratories. This means that the textbooks which subordinate energetics to physics will have to be rewritten to put energetics as the universal concept and physics as a subdivision. Such rewriting, when it comes about, will only be a beginning of a long and slow readjustment. The feeling of the finality of physical law, even of a mechanistic order, in the universe is something like a religion in the modern scientific world. In the past no other elementary principle except a physical one has been recognized by the scientist in making up his universe. The brilliant achievement of the physical sciences and technologies has naturally led to an enthusiastic over-optimism about the eventual outcome of a full explanation in such terms.

But now the facts of parapsychology are available for those who are detached enough to want them, available to those who want to go on past these modest beginnings to see what this other side of man and the universe may be like and to see what other principles may be found—beside this concept of nonphysical energetics—that help make human personality uniquely what it is.

*   *   *   *   *   *

While the nonphysical character of the psi process is mainly responsible for the resistance to the acceptance of psi by the other sciences, there is a comparably great difficulty inherent in the process itself—one that makes the ability difficult to work with. It is this difficulty that has been mainly responsible for the retarded appearance of psi research on the pages of science. Psi is, in fact, the most elusive phenomenon known to psychology; it is even difficult to capture and retain for purposes of continued and repeated study. Because of this handicap the kind of procedures which have made the other sciences advance rapidly are not available to this one. The fugitive character of psi has denied to parapsychology the possibility of easily repeatable demonstration and the consequent elaborate research designs which have helped other sciences so immensely. This difficulty is, of course, due to the nature of psi. So the research worker had to *learn* how to recapture psi phenomena under experimental conditions even while designing tests to prove that he had it and while he studied methods to improve the subject's performance. But every item of information about the place of psi in the psychological and biological branches contributes something to the eventual control and application and even the repeatable demonstration of the ability.

The importance of learning to control psi was recognized at an early stage at the Duke Laboratory. Actually, in point of time, it was recognized as an area of supreme interest as soon as the independence of ESP from space-time relations seemed to be pretty well indicated. The beginning researches on the psychology of psi went beyond mere looking for *individuals* having unusual psi ability to a search for classes or general types. Could a "psychic type" or a parapsychical personality classification be identified? Exploratory searchings began and for a time dominated the research at Duke. As the publications of the 1930's, 1940's, and 1950's reveal, the search ranged over a wide variety of groupings, some of them casual, perhaps depending upon advantages of location. As all explorations are likely to appear to later inspection, there is here too a certain lack of nicety in programming. The individual explorer's interest was often a determinant. Someone wanted to work with blind children and compare them with orphanage children of similar age. Another, or more than one, began racial comparisons. Still others went into mental hospitals to test for ESP among various classifications of mental disorder.

And all the while, by generalizing from the cumulative results, comparisons could be made as to the ability registered by the two sexes, by different age levels, and between numbers of other casual or natural groups. A growing vigilance for possible leads to a rich vein of psi ability can be noted. One of these explorations led to the effort to work with all the practicing mediums possible. Another group to receive special attention consisted of mental patients who believed themselves to be persecuted by telepathic influence; still another interest led into the anthropological literature to see if it might be especially profitable to work with a special culture if it seemed to give evidence of outstanding psi capacity. Various practices were explored which might involve psi abilities, as for example dowsing.

The coverage of these many levels and varieties of exploration was very considerable, though necessarily limited, too, in many ways. But the accumulative judgment of the years has led to the acceptance of the working hypothesis that psi capacity is very widespread in the human race. It would seem most likely to be part of the species heritage. This is especially suggested by the wider frequency of "good subjects" found in tests of very young children than in tests of older people. The difficulty of being at all confident that latent ability is being tapped by any given test makes it unwise to conclude anything from negative results. It seems likely that careful preparation and improvement of test methods could bring evidence of ESP out of everyone. The great variation found in individuals (and individual variation is, of course, not confined to parapsychology) is the cause of difficulties in getting their maximum ESP performance.

At this stage of thinking it seemed important to look at other species of animals to see if any signs of psi ability could be found. Initial interest in the question was strengthened by a survey of field studies on animal life involving migration and homing and a collection of stories about animals, mostly domesticated ones. Many very great puzzles were found in the biological literature, especially with regard to unusual cases of homing. With regard to migratory movements, also, great challenging mysteries remain. Animals perform many remarkable feats which lack any known and adequate explanation except ESP. This is enough to justify further inquiry even while it is not enough for a conclusion. Among a number of types of unusual and unaccountable animal behavior which could be explained by ESP are cases of unusual behavior of pet animals. In the most striking of these, a pet animal is separated from its human companions by accident or design and left behind when the family moves to another location at a considerable distance. In many cases the dog or cat has found its master after months of wandering over what are in some cases very long distances.

These hints from field studies led to experimental studies on certain species of animals that could best be subjected to ESP test situations. A sufficient amount of work with dogs, cats, and pigeons was done to give moderately good confirmation of the impressions gained from the field work and from anecdotal material. That which derived from dogs and cats was particularly impressive because these researches lent themselves better to laboratory control and the results were therefore more reliable. Only the extremely high standards of evidence and interpretation which this new field demands have restrained parapsychologists from the conclusion that these animals do show psi ability. There is a reasonably good case for that conclusion, but it can well be left for further support through more extensive work and by further independent confirmation. That man inherited his psi capacity from a long series of evolutionary ancestors will indeed be a valuable point to establish.

On the other hand, the biology of psi, like biology itself, has many good questions to which there are as yet no answers worth considering. While psi ability, to be as widespread as it is, must be considered a part of the hereditary endowment of the individual, we cannot yet decide conclusively whether or not it is a lost, or even a declining, ability. The suggestion is that when a dog or cat does appear to exercise ESP orientation, it shows a performance superior to anything so far encountered in the human species. This indicates that psi ability in man may have been suppressed in the evolution of his superior brain development. The idea, however, is as yet only a hypothesis.

The Duke researches have not yet touched in any significant way on the question of whether there is a localization in brain or body for the exceptional gift of ESP; whether there is a reception center equivalent to a sense organ or a brain center such as has been identified for visual or motor functions, we have as yet no clue. On the other hand, there is no reason to expect such localizations. The analogies with the sensorimotor system have mostly been wrong for ESP.

* * * * * *

Quite naturally, more progress has been made in finding a place for psi in the psychological organization of man than in the biological. In the search for a psychological understanding of parapsychical capacity, the explanation for the characteristic instability of psi was relatively soon discovered. One of the first observations, even in the earliest Duke experiments, was that under certain psychological conditions subjects in tests tended to show results below the average expected from chance; for example, when a subject was held to a testing schedule beyond the time he had expected to give to the task, or when a run of tests was made unduly and monotonously long. Again, if two types of test were being compared in the same experiment, one was likely to score above chance average and the other just as much below. Eventually it dawned upon the investigators that in scoring below chance the subject was avoiding the target with some consistency, even while he was in all probability consciously trying to score high. Then, too, it was observed that under repeated questioning of many different subjects, most of them could not give an insightful account of how it was that they were able to produce their best results. They did not know the difference between success and failure. The subject's response was made in the form of guessing, and he was quite unconscious of whether or not his guess was correct. Or if he succeeded, he was quite unconscious of that fact, as well as of how he brought it about. It was a most illuminating discovery about the psychological nature of psi to recognize that it lacks the introspective awareness that accompanies most sensory experience, especially since the lack applied equally well to all types of the phenomena. This was one of the first general psi characteristics recognized.

The fact that psi, in its essential operation, is unconscious and appears to be irrecoverably so has a great deal of significance. First, it is reasonable to ascribe to this fact about it much of the difficulty in exercising control over it. It is likely that the unconsciousness of the function is responsible for the inability of the subject to improve his efficiency by training. The same unconsciousness definitely limits the exercise of control over the demonstration of psi.

At the same time, the literature and understanding of the psi process are greatly enriched by this knowledge of the unconscious level of psi operation. Once the process was recognized as falling in this category, psi could be linked with a number of other forms of experience, particularly those through which it functions in reaching expression. By the study of case material and by the introspection of subjects in their test performance, it became clear that the psi function had to utilize forms of mental processes that normally had nothing to do with ESP or PK. ESP would appear in dreams, as intuitions, and in hallucinations. These were forms of familiar experience, but through them knowledge acquired by ESP was brought to consciousness. Even spontaneous physical manifestations have come to be regarded as an additional form of expressing a message or bit of knowledge extra-sensorially acquired. The fact that psi lacks any specific form of its own requires that it be translated into these forms already familiar in non-psi experience. This realization suggested again, as in the survey of biological findings, that psi was a primordial mode of communication, antedating the specialized sensorimotor system and preceding also the stage of conscious experience.

Fortunate it was, however, that workers in parapsychology had taken to the use of cards and dice for the measurement of ability. These methods and the mathematics long ago developed for applying the "laws of chance" to games (laws which apply equally well to psi tests) provide a definite base line known as "chance average" or "mean chance expectation." This is a dividing line from which the extent to which the scoring rate deviates can be measured. The measurement of the amount of deviation is a relatively simple, routine matter.

Special advantage was taken of the fact that this method is quite as useful and reliable in measuring a subject's ability to *avoid* the targets in a psi test as to hit them. It was discovered quite by accident, as has already been mentioned, that under certain conditions subjects will score below chance average to a significant (or extrachance) degree. That means that an explanation is called for; or, better still, it means that something about psi ability is being revealed. Without this method, which permits the ability to cut both ways, positively and negatively, above and below the chance mean, it would never have been discovered that psi ability is quite prone to this reversal of direction of deviation. It had to be given a name and is now called "psi-missing" as contrasted with normal psi-hitting. A large share of the research reported in the last two decades has to do with this peculiar psi-missing quirk, but it was only discovered because the test method was incidentally one that *could* show it. It is now a distinctive enough method to deserve a wider use (as well as a name) than is given to it in parapsychology alone.

This discussion of psi-missing brings us back again to the unconscious nature of psi. As a matter of fact, it seems unlikely that psi-missing would occur if psi were a conscious process. The working assumption has come to be that it is because of the unconscious level on which the subject's response is made that he is unaware of his success and failure. Because of this he unknowingly falls into the peculiar twist of response that makes him avoid the target he is trying to identify.

And yet, with all this unconsciousness, there is no doubt of a large voluntary role in the direction of the subject's effort. While in spontaneous experiences there is usually no conscious anticipation or desire for the experience, in the experiments, the subject goes through his tasks of trying to identify cards that are concealed from him or consciously *tries* to influence the fall of dice to make them turn up with designated faces as targets. Even though he does not know when, or even whether, he is succeeding (since he is being kept in the dark as to his success), he goes through the processes of "willing" to succeed or imagining that he is succeeding, as if he were playing a gambling or guessing game. Yet he definitely has in mind a certain target face in the dice-throwing test, and he definitely makes conscious choices of symbol order when he is calling cards in a test of clairvoyance or precognition, so that, practically, it may be said that an element of voluntary action is required. It has been considered a strange but nevertheless firmly settled point that, although psi is unconscious, it is also subject to conscious

direction as to its aim and even its timing. A subject may aim at a particular card selected out of a designated pack. The whole process of performance in the test calls for intelligent, structured, voluntary behavior on the part of the subject. Since this procedure works, it shows definitely that the ability involved is subject to those general characteristics of volitional mental life. Indeed, it carries the conception of psi very far into the factual picture of general psychology, and there are many features of the psi process in operation that are analogous to the more familiar processes of the mind. The role of motivation in spontaneous and experimental psi seems to be much the same as in all behavior. There are other generalizations, more or less clear-cut, that cover the parapsychical and the psychological in general.

The real difference comes in when the comparison is made with sensorimotor functions. Here, of course, the reliance of the sensorimotor system upon physical mediation between subject and object introduces a fundamental difference.

In summing up, it can be seen that the serious difficulty the parapsychologist encounters in eliciting his phenomena is due partly to the fact that the subject is generally unconscious of the operation. Under certain conditions which are now pretty well known, but by no means controllable, the subject may be thrown quite unknowingly into a psi-missing type of response. Or he may go through part of his test session or even through a single run with the first half on the positive side of the mean and the second half below mean chance expectation. He thus, of course, cancels out one deviation with the other. There are many other ways too in which, because of the psi-missing tendency and the unconsciousness of the process, the subject can so distort his responses as to obscure the effect when only the routine measurements are made. He may, for example, displace by hitting systematically on a neighboring target.

When the search began for psychological types who might

be outstandingly good performers in psi tests, it was found that when these types were classified by standard psychological methods, the general trend was for one end of the scale to correspond to high performance in the ESP tests and the other end to correspond to ESP scoring as far below the mean as the other end was above.   In other words, what the psychological test did was to separate the psi-hitters from the psi-missers, showing that the psi-hitting and psi-missing tendencies, as had been suspected from the beginning, were not included in human nature just as part of psi ability.   The psi-missing factor was discovered in human nature by psi-testing, that is true, and it allowed itself to be singled out and differentiated by a number of standard personality tests.   It was like a temperamental guard who stood at the door and decided whether ESP would exit walking forward or walking backward.

While thus far psi-missing has been more trouble to the experimenter than it has seemed to be worth, it has nevertheless had to be dealt with.   It will have eventually to be controlled, of course, before psi itself is going to be controlled. It is because of it that ordinary methods of amplifying communication will not work with psi.   This tricky, unconscious, hidden factor is not the sort of thing to behave like the machinery of most communication systems.   Being beyond the conscious control of the subject, for the most part psi ability can work in reverse without a sign being given.   Because of this, the statistical methods of condensing small bits of information into measurable ones can not be used.   It all goes back to this unconscious unsteadiness of psi.   Hence, still more progress on the psychology of psi is needed before the stage of statistical control can be reached; yet it can be added that definite progress has already been made.

The best practical control of the psi-missing effect that has been achieved so far has been the introduction of the two-aspect, or differential response, method of testing.   It has been found that if a subject is participating in a test with two parts to it, such as two types of test condition, of target, or of technique, and when the two are used in contrast to each other, the subject tends to score above the chance mean on the one and below chance on the other. Thus, by depending on the measure of the *difference,* the experimenter can take advantage of this differential tendency to get a better indication of psi than he could get without the two-aspect comparison.

Over the ages, one of the consequences of the unconscious status of psi has been the development of a wide range of practices believed to involve that ability. One, of course, was the interpretation of dreams; another involved the controlled induction of hallucinations, as through the use of a crystal ball; still another consisted of the use of various automatisms such as dowsing, automatic writing, and the Ouija board. Somewhat related are the induced trance states, whether brought on by ritual or drugs or methods approximating modern hypnosis. All these have attracted the attention of psi investigators in the search for conditions favorable to psi performance. It is understandable now how the ESP function could readily and easily be implanted in any one of these practices. The variety of adaptation is almost certainly beyond estimate.

But the value for psi research of these modifications of consciousness, whether automatisms, dissociations, trances, or what not, would seem to be relatively slight. Aside from the possibility of facilitating the training of a subject for a more continuous kind of performance, more stability under conditions of testing or practice, or a more lasting interest in research participation, there does not seem to be any real virtue in these psychological devices. The best claim made for hypnosis itself is that it may be a means of motivating subjects or training them to more stable and enduring test performance.

It is only fair to say that in trying to find the place of psi in the psychological sciences, the limitations are by no means wholly on the side of parapsychology. Far too little is known of the unconscious side of mental life in general. In psychiatry or general psychology nothing in the way of methods comparable to those of parapsychology has been developed for use in the study of the unconscious personality. In classroom tests of ESP, parallels have already been found between negative deviations in ESP tests and failing grades in the class. This emphasizes the far-reaching significance which the kind of methodical exploration that has been carried out in the parapsychical segment of personality could have for other areas of unconscious mental life. For example, many surface resemblances among the phenomena and problems of parapsychology and psychiatry suggest that, although psi itself is not linked to psychopathology as such, the quantitative methods of research in the one field could have value in the other.

The place which eventually will be accorded psi in the field of psychology will have to be prepared by an expanded conception of that field. Current psychology is frankly physicalistic in its orientation, brain-centered or cerebrocentric in its conception of what is fundamental. The findings of parapsychology challenge this physicalistic orientation and justify the view that there is a reality about the mind not to be accounted for by the physicalistic cerebrocentric view. That is the reason why, if a psychocentric scheme of human personality is to find its place in the firmly established scientific psychology of the future, it will have to be on a broader basis than that science now possesses.

In view of this analysis, the inhospitality of academic psychology toward the results of the psi researches reduces to a natural defensive reaction—a defense against a major change.

5

Advancement Toward Control and Application[5]

A fairly stereotyped human reaction can be observed as people, lay or scientific, are confronted with challenging new ideas such as those which parapsychology presents. The first reaction is a defensive one. They try to make *fun* of it. When that wears out, they try to make *sense* of it. After a certain amount of that, there is a third stage: they try to make *use* of it. In a field like engineering, the transition through these three stages may come about fairly rapidly; in medicine, a few years—or at most a generation; in the sciences of the mind, however, history is not very encouraging. Much depends, of course, on how difficult it is to make sense of the new discoveries; that is, on how well they fit in.

Obviously, in parapsychology the third stage, that of practical application, requires a measure of control over the abilities involved. However, control over their operation, in

5. Delivered by Dr. Louisa E. Rhine.

turn, depends upon more knowledge about them than has thus far been secured. Naturally, increase in knowledge depends greatly upon the vigor and extent by which the investigations are pushed and pursued, and that, in turn, upon the importance felt about their potential significance. So the question of when psi ability will be controllable and therefore useful in a reliable way comes back to the question of how much its potential usefulness is appreciated in anticipation.

The Duke Laboratory has naturally been concerned with the advancement of a program of study that would increase the ability to control the phenomena. The ultimate significance and usefulness of the research findings have never been lost sight of, but throughout the history of the Laboratory practical application has not been considered to be an immediate objective. Control over the exercise of the psi process has, it is true, been a frankly desired objective from the moment that ESP was first established as a genuine occurrence. The earnest search for increased control was as much motivated, however, by the appreciation of the advantage it would give to the research worker in his further study of the process as by any other consideration. It was recognized, likewise, that increased control would mean acceleration of the rate of acceptance by the other sciences. In the background, of course, was the obvious—almost too obvious—fact that the control of psi, of the ability at its best, could usher in fantastic new ranges of application as perhaps no other discovery had done.

*   *   *   *   *   *

Practices, of course, do not usually wait for the stage of applied science. Numerous fields of practice exist that are far from having the support of one hundred percent scientific knowledge. Some of these, even licensed practices, have no scientific foundation of fact whatsoever, and others are hardly halfway to the ideal point required, let us say, for a practice like that of astronautical engineering.

A wide variety of practices in which capacities of parapsychical nature were assumed have prevailed throughout the history of mankind in all its cultures. We may note first the more formal religions; in these, the assumption of parapsychical powers and agencies are an essential part of the doctrine. Then there have been the nonreligious practices of mediumship, fortunetelling, and prophecy, as well as automatisms, such as dowsing and healing practices, which have been attributed to occult influences.

It has been part of a broadly conceived program of the Duke Laboratory to be always on the alert for all practices or individual practitioners who seem to promise something reliable for study. One of the earliest encounters involved a so-called mind-reading horse. The animal's performance gave evidence that sensory cues were a part of the training, but even with the elimination of these, a fair case could be made for telepathic transmission. However, after a time the telepathy was crowded out, apparently because the sensory elements afforded a more dependable basis of practice. The case, in a way, suggests (speculatively) what may have been the evolutionary history of ESP; namely, its suppression by sensory development.

Similarly, an offer of volunteer help from a well-known medium, already mentioned, gave the Laboratory an opportunity to investigate possible psi capacities underlying the practice of mediumship. The success with which psi capacities were demonstrated in this case also fell off with continued repetitive demonstration. This reminds us again of the fugitive character of the psi capacity.

The practice of locating underground water or other objects by a dowser with a forked twig is one of the most widespread and most enduring of those involving psi. Many investigations have been made of individual dowsers by different staff members using, for the most part, test procedures that afforded a reasonably high degree of control but were also adapted to field conditions. A general judgment could be rendered in favor of the presence of a moderate amount of psi ability in most of the cases investigated. The evidence is sufficient to warrant a further, more exhaustive research program involving this particular motor automatism. But, again, in most cases there was the usual falling-off of the ability as the tests were repeated for series of desirable length. The disinclination on the part of some dowsers to continue is perhaps a clue to the unspoken state of mind of those who did. Tests are recognizedly disruptive in any field of science. Nowhere, however, is this so important as it is in the investigations of the delicate processes of parapsychology.

These illustrations will do to represent current practices which are based on the assumption of psi. They have not led investigators of the modern period to single out the practitioners of any type as a particularly good section of humanity for use in continued research. Performers equally good have been found among those who had no practical experience before being tested. The practices themselves and the beliefs accompanying them tend to get in the way of research designs, although, for some research purposes, there may be an advantage in the supporting effect of these beliefs.

Another generalization might be made to the effect that psi, like all other human abilities, has had a very, very long test in the practical affairs of men. The very fact that so little of this kind of practice has persisted through the millenia and that none of it makes a first-rate case today in competition with the applied sciences conforms to the view which has come from the studies of parapsychology; namely, that psi ability is not reliable enough in its present natural state for dependable, practical use. As with the case of many another hidden phenomenon or spontaneous occurrence in nature, science will have first to search out the principles which make it happen when it does and discover the conditions that produce or inhibit it or even reverse its effect. Then and only then can knowledge produce a reliable form of practice.

*　*　*　*　*　*

A fairly large section of the work and progress of the Laboratory has had to do with the search for better ways of improving results in psi tests. In other words, we have been searching for control; that is, control of the amount of information communicated through some variation of, or influence upon, the psi function.

In this search the subject himself has been of first consideration. In the beginning years the general notion prevailed that unusually gifted subjects should be sought and singled out, on the assumption that perhaps only a few persons had ESP ability and the experimenter's first task was to find them. Searches were made through preliminary screening tests in which, perhaps, an entire class would be tested in the hope of finding even a single especially gifted individual. In this way the first good performer at the Duke Laboratory was discovered. Others were located by the reports they gave of having had spontaneous experiences.

As personality measurements came into vogue in psychology, a number of them were used with the aim of separating high-scoring ESP subjects from low-scoring ones. For example, it was found that extraverts scored higher than introverts; yet the introverts, by scoring below the chance mean, proved that they had the same order of ESP ability as the high-scoring extraverts. They had to have it in order to avoid the target. In general, the psychological tests only helped to separate positive deviators from negative. Such tests have contributed much to knowledge of the psi process but they did not give any help on the selection of good subjects. Of course, this need not be the final answer; it remains, perhaps, for parapsychologists to make up their own subject-selection tests if any of these are ever to prove effective.

Another of the approaches which was followed in the search for high-grade ESP performers was the investigation of popular beliefs about persons who are reputed to have unusual "psychic ability." For example, studies were made of blind children as compared with the seeing. The popular notion, too, that identical twins are highly gifted in telepathy was followed up. These and many similar possibilities were looked into, directly or with the aid of colleagues better situated for a particular investigation.

As has already been explained, the selection of subjects on the basis of these suggested criteria did not prove to be profitable. It became increasingly evident that psi capacity was not the monopoly of any special group. It seemed most probable that it was at least as widely distributed as the human species. There were differences in the individuals, and much was learned about the psychology of those who were likely to score on the positive side of the chance average as distinguished from those who were likely to score on the negative side (the psi-hitters and the psi-missers as mentioned earlier). But the psi-hitter in one experiment might be a psi-misser in another, as often happened. Eventually it was decided that good subjects are not born, but made; and the problem of improving performance in psi tests shifted to an attempt to provide the conditions that *make* one a good subject, even while granting that there are doubtless innate differences that may make it easier for some subjects to be developed than for others.

In the studies of the conditions that favor good performance it was found that strength of motivation was the most important. Simple comparative tests with rewards helped to establish this point. The social atmosphere of the test situation had much to do with activating the subject's interest, and this greatly depended upon the personality and skill of the experimenter.

Hypnosis could be used to advantage to help in developing

and preserving a favorable attitude. Also novelty, challenge, and encouragement helped to build up and maintain scoring levels.

One of the most interesting problems arises from the unusually high level of performance of an occasional individual (often a child) for only a limited and transient period. Such short-term splurges are due to psychological factors still unknown but presumably discoverable. This possibility helps to keep the research focused on the psychology of the psi function. An increasing variety of mental states or conditions has been found that separates a group of subjects into psi-hitters and psi-missers. Most certainly a major advance will result from solving the problem of psi-missing. This curious, unconscious avoidance reaction may take place in the very port of entry of psi, and its solution could lead to the discovery of the essential character of the ability.

One of the other types of approach to the control problem is the effort to use statistical methods of concentrating small bits of information into more recognizable magnitude. Early in the Duke work the effort was made to use repeated guessing of cards individually enclosed in sealed opaque envelopes to see whether a compounding of responses of a given type would occur and, if so, whether it would tell with relative certainty the true nature of the enclosed target. As already stated, the psi-missing factor plays havoc with this thoroughly logical approach. This factor, along with the fact that the operation of psi is unconscious and, in addition, that the subject's performance varies greatly as he goes through the test day after day, introduces irregularities that disqualify this repeated-guessing method taken alone. One of the Laboratory staff members, however, has developed a combination of the repeated-guessing technique with some other devices, so that the prospect of this method of control has been greatly improved.

Still another of the methods undertaken to overcome the

uncertainties in psi testing was that of developing standard schoolroom tests that could be repeated with a minimum of variation. Assuming that fifth- and sixth-grade students are much the same in any part of the country or even in different countries, or that the high-school student is as close to a standard social specimen as can be obtained, strong emphasis was given to a broad testing program for the schoolroom. The consistency of responses obtained was of an impressive order when considered against the background of parapsychology research. Such inconsistencies as were introduced seemed to derive more from the nature of the experimenters themselves than from subjects in the classrooms. The outstanding point is that an assured supply of dependable subjects is available in the schools. The availability of this population insures a relatively stable performance level for research programs of the future. This is a step toward control.

A few words about other approaches to the control problem will help one to appreciate its inclusiveness. One major effort is a return to the study of nature's own gift of information, spontaneous psi experiences. It stands to reason that much could be learned if the experiences as well as the persons to whom they occur could be brought under sufficient psychological analysis. But here the limitations of psychology itself are great. However, studies have begun and some results can be mentioned. For instance, the study of telepathy cases shows that the old concept of telepathy is inadequate—the idea that the message is sent to the percipient by an agent. On the contrary, in the majority of cases at least, the percipient is the active party. He gets the message whether or not the agent sends it. This revision of concept is changing the planning of current experiments. Also, the idea that an ESP subject needs to be prepared for ESP by being told he is doing an ESP test is coming to be discounted because of the very spontaneity of ESP experiences. In the latter no one is told or is aware beforehand that ESP is going to occur.

That change of viewpoint, too, is altering some of the approaches to experimental plans and procedures.

An earlier venture into the search for psi in animals provided another approach to the control problem. It was thought that if animals have psi ability, perhaps they can utilize it better than man. It may be less inhibited. It may be possible to experiment with it more freely and advantageously. There may be a "psi guinea pig." The investigation, though promising, was found to be slow and costly and demanding. It had to be allowed to await more extensive support and personnel.

Still another branch of inquiry aimed at improving control involves the attempt to measure psi on a level that does not depend on conscious response. When psi occurs in the unconscious, there may or may not be a concomitant conscious response. The conscious response may be secondary. The person may register a slight change in blood volume, or possibly a change in his electroencephalogram, or brain wave; there may be a slight change in the galvanic skin response or in some other physiological condition. None of these measures have yet been sufficiently tested to show whether they will be aids towards increased control. They have, however, introduced new potential for measurements. It is possible that in combination they may prove eventually to be reliable indicators of the operation of psi.

The search for special states or conditions already mentioned still goes on with the aim of finding favoring ones that may release the subject's latent ability. Passing over the automatisms and trances already mentioned, whether mediumistic or hypnotically induced, there are still a few others being kept in the focus of attention. The practice of yoga, with the mental and psychosomatic controls developed in that training, will be a subject of serious study. Also, the drugs that induce hallucinations, and the production and study of controlled dreams are lined up as part of the program of control studies, for the general aim is to leave unopened no door that fronts on the wide boundaries of this problem area.

As we all know, understanding falls into orderly systematic lines as knowledge accumulates and forms a rational network of theory. But the control of so elusive and deeply involved a process system as that of psi is not likely to yield to *one* of the approaches alone. It no doubt will depend rather on a combination of them. But for this ultimate stage, prepared minds are necessary; and in making the approaches mentioned, we are hoping to have them.

*   *   *   *   *   *

That control over psi capacity will come is reasonably certain. With what limitations and qualifications it will eventually be achieved, of course no one could know, just as no time schedule for it can be fixed. The kind of interest most likely to advance the research program to that high achievement will not come from neighboring professional fields, although presumably they, too, are dedicated to the understanding of man and his control of himself. The professions are bound too much by existing belief systems, and these are such as to prevent easy recognition of the potential importance of psi abilities.

Instead, the professional groups farthest away from parapsychology, those concerned over the affairs of men on the terrestrial scene, are showing the greatest and most uninhibited interest in the investigation of psi. The possibility that psi may be a mode of communication independent of space has interested technological people more than anything else about it. Far more have been interested from this angle than from that of the significance of psi for the understanding of man. This practical interest in psi among the space sciences is an entirely legitimate and proper one, and there is every reason to welcome it. But at the same time it must be recognized that its justification depends, not upon present knowledge, but upon the assumption of future advances in the field. As it is, the present state of knowledge is promising and sufficient to justify that interest. But certainly a lot of research will have to be done before psi can mean anything in astronautical engineering, or have any other practical application.

*   *   *   *   *   *

But we must separate the application of psi from the application of the fact that psi occurs. Once attention is directed to the realization that it is now firmly established as a human capacity and must be accommodated as part of the natural science of man and the universe, the findings of parapsychology become immediately useful as facts of nature without awaiting further developments in control and applicability except as these may affect the recognition of psi itself. It is no doubt true that the practical application of psi ability would do more than anything else to break down resistance to its acceptance by its scientific neighbors. Beyond any doubt the mere advance to a moderate degree of control over the ability would permit it to be demonstrated so impressively that the time of recognition of its significance would definitely be shortened.

The value of the mere fact that psi occurs stands out boldly enough when we ask what a man is—surely the most important question of all. But when this question is asked, it is necessary to specify a reference point and add, for example, "What is man with respect to the physical world? Or the biological world?" What man is with respect to physical nature is logically the first question to ask in a "qualitative analysis" of his natural composition. Parapsychology has found the answer in part—fragments of results that cannot be explained by physical law. So man is not wholly physical.

But since no other kind of basic causal principle beside the physical one has ever been claimed by the sciences, this finding that here is a process not entirely physical is revolutionary in the extreme. However, since it is now a firmly established finding, its effect upon all the many applied areas where the nature of man is important can hardly be overestimated. This revolutionary kind of bearing should be considered to be of the highest order of usefulness in a scientific discovery, one that modifies and corrects ways of thinking that prevailed before it became known. This corrective usefulness of the psi findings will, we know, be long in being fully recognized. *How* long will depend greatly upon the program of the Foundation we are celebrating today.

6

Closing Remarks

by Dr. J. B. Rhine

You have heard these reviews of the stages through which this new science has developed on the Duke campus. In the year ahead, this prelude to the future of parapsychology will be drawing to a close as the Duke Parapsychology Laboratory becomes the Institute for Parapsychology under the sponsorship of the Foundation.

But even as this transition to a stage of greater security, freer expansion, and widened responsibility takes place, all true friends of these studies must look back upon the decades of progress at Duke with gratitude to this great and growing institution. It has fostered a radically new branch of inquiry through the trials of its hardest years. It has, beyond all the other universities of its time, been generous to that foundling science. It has thereby set for its own traditions a notable example of hospitality to challenging ideas that are verifiable. Is there another American university that can equal this sponsorship of the unorthodox?

Some will ask, I know, "But could it happen here again?"

Less easily, perhaps, one may grant. Conventionalism grows upon us all with the years, especially upon institutions. But much will depend upon the example of the foster-child itself. We can at least give this example its greatest effectiveness by making parapsychology something the University will be proud to have sponsored.

Part II

Some Current Researches
in Progress at Duke

7

Introductory Remarks

by Dr. K. Ramakrishna Rao, Chairman

As we look ahead to the future of the Foundation, we logically ask the question: Can we acquire the competent personnel needed for the growing responsibility and extended coverage to be anticipated with the development of this new science?   It has been justifiable to look over the past, as the forenoon program helped us to do, in making an estimate of reasonable possibilities for the future.

But the present, too, has its value in pointing out what may be expected.   The brief review of the work of a section of present personnel-in-training to be offered in this afternoon's program should afford some basis of what may rightly be expected from the research worker of parapsychology in the future.   We may be well assured they will be the best trained and the most carefully selected yet in the history of this branch of inquiry.

The short papers to be given were "invited" without regard to whether the piece of work was finished or just begun.   The aim has been to afford a glimpse of the training program in action—not for its finished accomplishments, but for its signs of progress. The invited group consists of predoctoral psychologists who are currently in training at the Duke Laboratory.

The first of our participants this afternoon is Miss B. K. Kanthamani, a native of India. Miss Kanthamani is a trained clinical psychologist who was working at the All India Institute of Mental Health in Bangalore before she came to the Parapsychology Laboratory as a Visiting Research Fellow to prepare for a career in parapsychology. She will present to us the results of a series of her language ESP experiments. A more complete report of her research will be published, I believe, in the March, 1965, number of the *Journal of Parapsychology*.

Mr. James C. Carpenter will give us the second report. Mr. Carpenter, Summer Research Fellow at the Parapsychology Laboratory, a Stone Fund Scholar of the FRNM, and a former student at Duke, is now a graduate student in psychology at Ohio State University. His paper deals with his work on the possible relation between the defense mechanisms of his subjects and their ESP scores.

The third participant, Mr. Robert L. Morris, is a graduate student in psychology at Duke University and a Summer Research Fellow of the Parapsychology Laboratory. Mr. Morris has worked with an apparatus for testing PK (psychokinesis) designed and built by Mr. W. E. Cox of Southern Pines, North Carolina, and he will present the current results he has obtained with the "clock machine."

Mrs. Sara R. Feather is a graduate student in psychology at Duke. A former research assistant at the Parapsychology Laboratory, she is now a Stone Fund Scholar of the FRNM and a Summer Research Fellow at the Parapsychology Laboratory. She will give us a report of her experiments dealing with the correlation of memory and ESP.

The fifth paper in the program this afternoon will be given

by Mr. Rex Stanford, a graduate student in psychology at the University of Texas. Mr. Stanford, also a Summer Research Fellow, holds a Stone Fund Scholarship from the FRNM. His paper deals with explorations into possible relations between "brain waves" and ESP.

And, finally, there is a paper by Mr. Soji Otani from Japan. Mr. Otani is an Assistant Professor of Psychology at the Japanese Defense Academy. For the last ten months he has been at the Parapsychology Laboratory as a Visiting Research Fellow. Mr. Otani will tell us about his attempts to correlate the measurement of electrical resistance in the skin (GSR, or galvanic skin response) and success in ESP tests.

8

An ESP Experiment with Two-Language Targets

by Miss B. K. Kanthamani

The role and range of target material in ESP and PK tests have been matters of intensive study in recent years. Subjects were found to be successful with various kinds of symbols inscribed on cards and even with targets generated by computers. It has been found that such physical aspects of the targets as color, shape, size, and material do not seem to bear any limiting relation to the functioning of psi, while the subjects' psychological reactions to the targets do seem to be relevant to his success or failure. One of the findings in the target area is that when the subject is presented with two kinds of target material, he tends for some reason to respond differentially. In one study, for example, the subjects were asked to prepare cards bearing symbols, pictures, or drawings of their own choice. When these cards were used along with ESP cards, they obtained more hits than expected by chance with their own cards as targets and a lower number of hits than expected by chance with ESP cards. The difference between the rate of scoring on the cards of their own choice and on the ESP cards was statistically significant. It is important to note that ESP was occurring in that experiment on both kinds of targets but in opposite directions. This sort of opposite reaction in a dual-aspect test has been called the differential psi response.

The series of experiments to be reported here were undertaken to see whether this differential response would hold up from experiment to experiment in tests involving a language ESP situation. Dr. K. Ramakrishna Rao carried out a number of experiments using words in two languages as target material. He found that subjects responded differentially to the two langauges. The use of words in a foreign language was something new in ESP research and appeared to be challenging to the subjects.

Following Dr. Rao's work, I also used target words in two languages. One was English; the other was Hindi, known to the experimenter but not to the subjects. The target words were *Ball, Fish, Love, Peace,* and *Tree,* and their translations into Hindi.

In the first experiment 10 key cards bearing the five different words in English and Hindi were shown to the subject to give him a feeling of familiarity with the words. He thus had a chance to see the strange words before the test. Then, out of the subject's sight, one English and one Hindi key card were placed in each of five opaque black envelopes. These envelopes were placed in front of the subject. A mixed pack of 50 target cards, made up of one 25-card pack of English and one 25-card pack of Hindi word cards, was thoroughly shuffled and given to the subject. The cards were kept face-down, and the subject was asked to place them one by one opposite whichever key-card envelope he thought contained a matching card.

Ten subjects participated in this experiment. Each subject did four runs; that is, he made 100 trials or guesses. Thus there were, in all, 1000 guesses: 500 for English cards and 500 for Hindi cards. For each language, 100 would be expected to be correct by "chance" alone. The subjects in the first experiment obtained 117 hits on English cards and only 78 on Hindi cards. It may be noticed that the deviation from chance is larger on Hindi than on English, suggesting that ESP was operating even on Hindi, in which there were fewer hits. The difference in the rate of scoring between the English and Hindi targets is a result that would be expected to occur only once in 500 times by chance.

The second experiment was a group test, and so the procedure was different from the first. Each subject received a sealed opaque envelope containing a target sheet on which were written the different words in both languages arranged randomly. A record sheet was stapled to the outside of the envelope, and on this the subjects wrote their guesses, trying to match the appropriate words on the sheet inside.

Eight subjects were given this test, and they obtained 48 and 31 hits on English and Hindi respectively, with 40 hits expected by "chance." Even though the result of this small series is not as significant as the previous one, the average number of hits per run on English is higher than the average on Hindi, and the average number of hits on Hindi is lower than in the previous experiment.

The third experiment was similar to the second except that the subjects were tested individually. Here also the subjects obtained more hits on English than on Hindi targets.

When the probabilities of the three series were combined, the odds against chance were more than 1000 to 1. It is evident from this that ESP is manifest as a differential re-action in the experiment as a whole.

Apart from the significance of the raw ESP scores, there was a significant degree of consistency in the way the subjects responded to English and Hindi targets. The subjects scored 26 times in the expected direction (i.e., positively on English targets and negatively on Hindi targets) and only six times in the opposite direction. Here again the result would be expected by chance only once in a thousand such experiments.

These results give fresh evidence for the consistent operation of the differential response throughout the three series and their variations. Moreover, ESP seems to operate on the unknown as well as the known language, positively on English and negatively on Hindi. This does not mean, however, that the subjects crossed the language barrier in the strict sense, because they had an opportunity to familiarize themselves with the foreign-language words at the beginning of the test. Whatever may be the complete explanation as to why the subjects tended to guess the English words correctly and to avoid the Hindi words, it is my suggestion that they unconsciously felt it was hard to cross the language barrier or that English was easier, less baffling. In Dr. Rao's studies, his male subjects obtained significantly better scores on targets of the *unfamiliar* language, and he hypothesized that the novelty of a new language and the challenge of the language barrier provided additional motivation to his subjects. In retrospect it would seem as though there might have been a difference in the way Dr. Rao and I presented our tests. He may have presented his in a way that instilled confidence in at least his male subjects, whereas I, by unwittingly emphasizing their unfamiliarity with Hindi, may have contributed to the subjects' preference for English. It is of interest to discover these delicate influences that affect ESP success and to observe that they can operate consistently from one series to another. Gathering such knowledge should enable us eventually to learn to control this ability.

9

An Exploratory Test of ESP in Relation to Anxiety Proneness

by Mr. James C. Carpenter

This is an account of a small study done in the Parapsychology Laboratory by the Swedish psychologist Mr. Martin Johnson and myself, inquiring into the possible relationship between a subject's ESP scoring rate and the degree of perceptual defensiveness characteristic of the individual.

When two sets of measurements are being compared, it is well to have some discussion about what is being measured.

The construct of major interest in this experiment is, of course, extrasensory perception—more specifically, clairvoyance. Clairvoyance has been defined in general as "the extrasensory perception of objective events as distinguished from the mental activities of another person." Clairvoyance, we may say, is indicated when a person exhibits knowledge of the objective world in conditions which exclude the possibility of his having gained the knowledge through sensory contact or telepathy. The exact procedures used for measuring clairvoyance in this study will be discussed a little later; but first a few words about our second construct, perceptual defensiveness and the DMT (Defense Mechanism Test) method.

One can approach the problem of understanding the meaning of an experimental psychological concept in several ways. He can examine the theoretical structure in which it performs a function; he can search his memory for human experiences which might have given rise to the exact operations used in measuring it.

The psychoanalytic theory of Sigmund Freud provides the context for the construct used here, and perhaps we may say that the common and puzzling phenomenon often called "self-deception" is its most important experimental touchstone.

Freud's theorizing was built largely out of his observations of neurotic individuals, persons who somehow have less than the ordinary ability to live happily, successfully, and co-operatively in their societies. Freud's neurotic person grapples, on the one hand, with a troublesome stream of "inner" events, impulses, and ideas, and, on the other, with the threatening world of external reality. The battle is waged in that buffer zone just outside the realm of consciousness and the individual's weapon is what Freud called the "defense mechanism." Of the latter there are two main types: utter rejection from consciousness of the impulse or stimulus, and distortion of it. Freud catalogued specific types of mechanisms which are employed in this way, such as reaction formation, projection, denial. With these concepts we all have some familiarity. The steam which fuels these machines of misrepresentation, Freud dubbed "anxiety"; and in this strictly Freudian meaning of the term we may say that this test, which measures the employment of defense mechanisms, measures anxiety.

All of us have noticed the phenomena of self-deception in others if not in ourselves. For instance, an over-talkative person may be known to hear not a word of the hints aimed at steering him to some more meditative activity such as reading the encyclopedia or taking a stroll. People differ in their tolerance for threatening events; one way of expressing intolerance is simply not to perceive, either correctly or at all, what knocks on the door of consciousness.

The DMT was developed by Dr. Ulf Kragh of the University of Lund to measure the degree to which a person perceives the events in his world and in his own viscera with this sort of tolerance or intolerance. The apparatus used in his test is a tachistoscope, a projector which can flash pictures on a screen for different durations, beginning with exposures far too short for conscious discriminative perception. The picture that is used is that of a boy holding a violin and obviously engaged in pleasant reveries. Just over the boy's shoulder, however, oddly suspended in air, skulks a gentleman of apparently unkind intentions. These two are called, respectively, the "hero" and the "threat." This picture is flashed before the subject in a series of exposures of increasing length. After each exposure the subject is instructed to draw a picture of what he saw, along with a written description. Defensiveness is taken to be indicated by the number of exposures it takes for the subject to report correctly the peripheral threat and by the number and types of ways in which he has distorted his interpretation of either the hero, or the threat, or both, in the direction of diluting or misdirecting the element of threat. Rest assured, as odd or harmless as Mr. Threat might seem when viewed in a large lump, when flashed to the preconsciousness in small doses, he is enough to make at least some of us draw for our defense mechanisms like so many John Waynes or Matt Dillons.

In the summer of 1963, Mr. Martin Johnson, student and fellow-researcher with Dr. Kragh, was invited to visit the Parapsychology Laboratory. He came with the idea that people who are prone to draw their preconscious blinds in matters of visual perception might act somehow similarly toward perceptions which are extrasensory. This was a good hypothesis, as Johnson knew, in terms of previous ESP work in which a search had been made for relationships between subject characteristics and ESP success. Such work has come to be a focus of attention because of the problem of psi-missing, that is, scoring below mean chance expectation. When such negative scoring is mixed indiscriminately with the results of positive scoring, the average score looks like no ESP at all. The problem of reliably separating factors making for psi-hitting and psi-missing is a major one, fundamental to further progress. Some good starts have been made. Schmeidler and workers following her lead have found that persons who believe ESP to be possible tend to be psi-hitters (that is, to score above chance expectation) and that people who do not believe in that possibility tend in the opposite, psi-missing, direction. There is a clear analogy here to the work on sensory perception, where belief that a stimulus could occur has been shown to facilitate its accurate perception.

Other work strikes some harmonious chords with the DMT hypothesis. Studies by Humphrey, Shields, Nicol, Schmeidler, and others give indications that ESP is positive in subjects describable as extraverted, not-withdrawn, self-confident, nonaggressive, and well-adjusted socially. Psi-missing was found more often in subjects with the opposite characteristics. There are no exact fits to be made here with the DMT rationale, but one does sense some harmony.

Agreeing that Johnson had a fine idea, three researchers, all of whom were about to begin very different ESP experiments, agreed to use the same subjects, rank them in terms of the quality of their ESP performances, and compare these rankings with the ones obtained by Mr. Johnson using the subjects' DMT performances. An overall average ESP ranking was also to be computed later, and this also was to be compared with the ranking by DMT.

In two of the three results, striking associations of a

strength scarcely imputable to coincidence were found. And the association, happily, was the expected kind; that is, people who were relatively high in perceptual defensiveness were relatively low in ESP-hitting, and vice versa. The association between the average ESP ranking and DMT ranking was in the same direction and of similar strength.

My ESP experiment was one of the two which yielded the strong and expected result. Ten local high-school students served as subjects. All of them claimed to believe that ESP was a possibility, and all appeared eager to do well. An ESP card technique called "blind matching" was used wherein four opaque envelopes, each containing one out of four ESP symbols (star, circle, cross and square) were placed before the subject. He was given a deck of cards of the same symbols, face down, and told to place them one by one, without looking at them, on top of the envelopes containing the target cards, with the intention of matching the symbols together. This is something like putting the A papers in the A file, the B papers in the B file, and so on, except in the dark. As it turned out, good filers had also coped pretty well with Mr. Threat when faced by him.

High ESP went with low defensiveness, and vice versa. Each subject performed 10 runs of ESP tests, sorting 40 cards per run. Thus there were 400 trials for each subject. Sometimes all 10 runs were done in one sitting, sometimes in two. Each run was scored immediately after it was finished so that the subject could learn how well he was succeeding as the experiment progressed. An average of the 10 scores was calculated for each subject, and these averages served to rank the persons by their demonstrated ESP success. It was this ranking which was compared with the DMT ranking arrived at independently by Mr. Johnson. The Pearson formula for correlation of rank orders was used, and a correlation coefficient of .79, with 9 degrees of freedom, was obtained. A coefficient of this size or larger would occur by chance in fewer than one of every hundred such experiments performed. Thus, the hypothesis of coincidence can be said to be reasonably excluded.

It is difficult to be neat and specific about the end of the story of a piece of research. This is so largely because every such ending, if the study has been worth its ESP cards, is itself a beginning—of another, or another dozen, experiments. Any good result suggests at least its weight in better questions. Some of the major ones from this study which must be carefully and systematically asked are: What aspects do the two successful experiments have in common that could be tested as contributing to the effect? How could one best go about repeating the experiment without changing any important factors to an important degree? Is the utilization of any specific defense mechanism associated more strongly with ESP than any others? Would similar comparisons with other measures of defensiveness or anxiety produce similar results? If the ESP targets were constructed out of threatening figures rather than geometric designs, would the effect be stronger? (For instance, one could make a deck of cards out of, say, the Creature from the Black Lagoon, Khrushchev, some critic of ESP research, and a certain candidate for the presidency.) The questions could be multiplied indefinitely. In the future lies the aim of constructing trustworthy generalizations about the ESP phenomenon. Each step, such as the one I have reported, may be a contribution; and each step makes for exciting work.

10

The Measurement of PK (Psycho-kinesis) by Electric Clock

by Mr. Robert Lyle Morris

Until a few years ago, almost all of the research done on psychokinesis, or PK, involved relatively large objects in motion, such as dice, coins, and so on, which the subject would attempt to influence or manipulate in accordance with a pre-arranged pattern chosen for him by the experimenter. Such methods gave a lot of information about some of the ways in which PK operated. It was found that large dice work just as well as small dice and that many dice thrown simultaneously work just as well as, if not better than, a few dice. Such results indicated that PK effectiveness apparently is not influenced by the amount of physical energy involved, nor by the complexity of the task.

Recently, however, much work has been done with methods other than dice-throwing in an effort to find out more about the physical nature of the PK process itself. One of the main researchers in this area has been Mr. William E. Cox, of Southern Pines, N. C. This afternoon I am going to tell you about the work some of us have been doing with two of his PK test devices, the "two-clocks machine" and the "one-clock machine."

The two-clocks machine is composed essentially of two one-handed, electric timing clocks hooked up to an electro-mechanical randomizing apparatus. Each time the subject presses a button, the hands on each clock move a certain distance. The precise distance each hand travels depends on the randomizing apparatus. The subject's task is to try to exert a PK influence on the machine and make the hand on one of the clocks (the target clock, which the subject can see) go farther than or not so far as—according to which task is prescribed—the hand on the other clock (which only one experimenter sees). Each trial consists of a clockwise swing followed by a counterclockwise swing, thereby giving the subject two chances to make good.

For each experimental run, the subject is asked to draw the bottom one of a stack of sheets presented to him in a folder. This sheet gives him directions as to which way he should try to influence the clock hands. Sixteen pairs of letters are written on each sheet, eight reading "FS," meaning "fast-slow" (that is, the subject is to try to make the hand go farther in the clockwise direction than in the returning, counter-clockwise direction), and eight "SF" pairs of letters, meaning "slow-fast" (or that the subject is to try to make the hand go not so far out in the clockwise direction but farther coming back in the counterclockwise direction).

After the subject has completed each run, the sheet he has used is returned to the top of the stack of sheets in the folder. This procedure guards against the possible influence of pre-cognition on the part of the subject or experimenter when it comes time to choose directions for the run. The experi-menters do not see the letters on the direction sheet until after the run is over and the final clock readings are compared with the directions given the subject.

Two experimenters are used in the experiment, one to

score for each clock. Neither one can see both clocks at the same time, and neither knows the subject's target. This reduces the possibility of making scoring errors that could favor the subject, provides a double check on the scoring, and all but rules out the possibility of the experimenter's own PK influence on the machine. Thus, it is an advance in technique for PK research.

In scoring, the final two readings of the clocks are compared. If the target-clock hand is farther clockwise than the other clock's hand and if the subject's instructions on the sheet were to make the target hand go out faster and return slower, then he has a hit. Similarly, if the target hand goes farther counterclockwise than the hand of the other clock, and if the instructions were to make the target hand go out slower and return faster, the subject gets a hit. Otherwise, in both cases, he gets a miss.

The one-clock machine operates in a similar way. It consists of one timing clock hooked up to a mechanical, rather than electromechanical, randomizing apparatus. The procedure is essentially the same, except that in scoring hits or misses, the final position of the clock hand and its distance from its own starting point, the zero mark, are noted instead of its position relative to another clock hand.

In both machines, the focal point which is theoretically influenced by PK is in the randomizing apparatus itself, rather than the hands of the clocks, which serve only to indicate in a measurable way what goes on in the randomizing devices.

Also, in the work with either machine, each run contains 16 pairs of "fasts" and "slows" on each direction sheet. By chance alone a subject would be expected to get 50 per cent hits, or 8 out of 16.

Now we come to some of the results obtained with these machines. So far, the main work with them has been preliminary and exploratory, but at this time it can be said that both machines have given results that show PK. While hits are to be expected 50 per cent of the time by chance alone, with both of these machines subjects have been averaging around 53 per cent success. This includes work conducted by Mr. Cox, by Mr. James Carpenter and Mrs. Sara Feather, by Mrs. Ruth Klopper and myself, and by Miss B. K. Kanthamani and myself. Several of the series run by Mr. Cox and one by Mrs. Feather and Mr. Carpenter gave statistically significant results. My own series have not yet shown overall significance, but my percentages of success have been similar to those of Mr. Cox. Much more work along these lines will have to be done.

Of additional interest is the fact that in the one-clock machine occasionally the clock hand will come to rest exactly on zero, thus making neither a hit nor a miss. In such cases the subject gets a second chance on that particular trial and is asked to do it over again. On such second chances, the percentage of success for all data checked so far is over 60 per cent. These trials alone approach statistical significance, suggesting that a subject may put forth a special effort on these second chances. The same suggestion comes from another source. The greater the deviation from zero in the one-clock machine (or the greater the difference between the hands on the two-clock machine), the larger the percentage of hits has tended to be (approximately 60 per cent).

Also, in the two-clocks machine the electromechanical randomizing apparatus contains several electrical relays. For each subject, one relay was in operation half the time, and four relays were in operation the other half. Neither the subject nor the experimenters knew until afterward how many relays were involved on a given trial. So far there has been no significant difference between success on one relay and success on four relays.

Several other ways of looking at the data have been used, and plans for further research with these machines are being developed. All in all, we feel that the clock machines offer a promising new tool for looking a bit more closely at the psychokinetic effect and what makes it tick.

11

A Comparison of Performance in Memory and ESP Tests

by Mrs. Sara R. Feather

I have been interested in comparing subjects' scores on ESP tests with their scores on a memory test because we need to know more about how ESP is related to other mental processes in order to better understand what it means and how to control it.

The basic procedure used for this comparison is this: A subject, a high-school student for instance, is shown a list of ESP symbols or digits which he views for 15 or 20 seconds. He is told that in a few minutes he will be asked to recall the order of these symbols as best he can. During those few minutes, he is given another task. This time he is asked to guess the order of some other randomized ESP symbols which he has not had the opportunity to see.

Now the question is Will there be a relationship between these two different tasks, the first a test of his memory and the second a standard ESP test? To score well on the first he needs to have learned a fairly difficult order of symbols and the correct location of this ordering within an unstructured list, and he must have retained some of this learning over a period during which he is dealing with the same symbols in a different manner. To score well on the ESP test he will have to name the correct order of more of the symbols than would be expected by chance. If nothing but chance operates on both tasks, the scores should average about five correct in each 25 trials, both on the memory and the ESP tests. This would mean that there was only an accidental relationship between the scores on the two types of tests. If, on the other hand, there should appear to be a significant relationship between these scores, it would suggest that memory and ESP are both being measured and are related in this experimental situation.

In two series of experiments conducted last summer, I got the first suggestion that there indeed might be such a relationship. In that work there seemed to be a tendency for subjects who scored low on a memory test (that is, five or below) to score below chance on the ESP tests too. Because these two particular series had not been planned with such a comparison in mind, this was just a suggestion, but it initiated a series of tests to study the problem directly. Since then, there have been two series of tests replicating the earlier work, each adding evidence of a relationship between ESP ability and the ability to recall and indicating in particular that low scorers on the one task are low scorers on the other. (As is our standard procedure, of course, each series of tests was planned in advance as to number of subjects, number of trials per subject, and other procedural matters necessary to ensure the exclusion of extraneous factors which might influence the results.)

Because the objective was to compare memory and ESP, the tests were made fairly similar in form. For each, the chance baseline was the standard one used in ESP tests whereby, on the average, five correct hits are expected out of 25 trials. This allows for the possibility—which turns out to be very important in these studies—that subjects may score below the chance baseline. When subjects consistently score below chance to a significant degree in ESP tests, we suspect that they must somehow be avoiding the correct target. We call this "psi-missing"; but when this type of score occurs in a memory test, some other explanation, such as blocking or repression, may be necessary. Such speculation is premature, however, and is mentioned in passing as an example of one of the questions which is being raised by this study.

In the planning of each new series so far, small changes have been introduced for the purpose of making the memory test more difficult, and hence of obtaining a greater proportion of low- *versus* high-memory subjects, since it is these who have shown the interesting relationship. By reducing the viewing time or increasing the number of ESP guesses in the waiting period before recall, the attempt was made to accentuate the relationship between low-memory and low-ESP scores.

Now about the results: The correlational analysis of the overall results for the four series (the two last year and the two replications this year) suggests that there is a direct relationship between the two processes being measured. The chance probability for this effect is about 2 in 100, with all four series showing the same consistent relationship. When a subject recalls a relatively large number of ESP symbols correctly from those he has seen, he is likely to have made a relatively large number of ESP hits on the card symbols he has never seen. And if he recalls only a few symbols correctly, he is likely to have guessed only a few correctly on the ESP tests.

One of the standard methods of analysis is that of comparing the number of low ESP scores with the number of high ESP scores which subjects make with relation to whether they are low or high on the memory test. This type of analysis shows in the most clear-cut way that there is a difference in the ESP scoring of the 56 subjects who comprise the four series, depending on whether they are high or low on their memory test. The probability is only 9 in 1000 that such a relationship would be shown by chance; that is, that the low-memory subjects would obtain such a preponderance of low ESP scores and such an absence of high ESP scores in contrast to the opposite scoring by the high-memory subjects.

Another way of viewing the results is in terms of how each subject as a person averaged on one type of test as compared with the other type of test. Of the 37 people whose scores on the memory test were such as to call them "high memory," 16 averaged above chance on their ESP tests, 5 of them averaged right on the chance line, and 16 others averaged below chance. If only these high-memory people were involved, no relationship with ESP would be shown on this basis. But when the 19 people who comprise the low-memory group are considered, it appears that only three of them averaged above chance on their ESP scores. Sixteen of this group (84%) averaged below chance. The probability that these results from the total 56 subjects would occur by chance is about 4 in 100.

The overall results obtained so far give fairly clear indication that, for some reason, subjects tend to score with similar success in their memory, or recall, of symbol order and their ability to guess the order of symbols not seen.

Obviously there are more questions raised than answered at this stage of the work, and further work will continue on these questions this summer. One problem which may need study concerns the below-chance scores on the memory test. We have often speculated that there should be analogues to "psi-missing" in other psychological processes if we could but measure them, and it is possible that below-chance memory may be one of these.

The main point which the present work suggests to me, however, is that if a measure can be obtained of an independent factor (such as a memory score) which is known to correlate with ESP scores in a particular situation, it will be a step toward predicting what a subject's ESP scores will be.

12

A Study of the Relationship Between ESP Scoring and "Brain Waves"

by Mr. Rex G. Stanford

E very day those who are in contact with parapsychology seem to be hearing more and more about
the relation of ESP and physiological variables, such as brain
waves, the electrical resistance of the skin, or circulatory
changes. Indeed, this kind of study is receiving much emphasis at the present time. Here at the Parapsychology
Laboratory, for example, three persons have for some time
been actively engaged in the study of three different physiological factors as related to ESP. There are many good
reasons for this priority being given physiological measures.
One of the key reasons is that such studies could very well
play an important role in the task of bringing psi under
control.

If, for instance, by recording physiological changes in a
subject we can know with a fair degree of accuracy when he
is responding by ESP and when he is not, we will have ESP
under a very real degree of control. In addition, these studies
may give good clues as to what bodily systems are involved

in psi, how psi is brought into conscious experience and action, and maybe even some indications of how we can more directly encourage or control the psi processes.

These are some of the goals aspired to in the combined study of physiology and psi. These long-range goals are important enough that we will not want to abandon this approach even though it may, by utilizing the fine tools of modern technology, require much in the way of technical knowledge, careful planning, and persistence.

In neurophysiology there is one tool which at various times since its inception has been associated with the study of ESP. This is the electroencephalogram, the so-called brain wave recorder, or EEG. This device, first created and used by Hans Berger in Germany in 1929, records on graph paper minute electrical changes occurring in the brain. It records them by the application of electrodes to the scalp and the amplification of the electrical changes existent at the scalp that result from the ever-present ebb and flow of electrical potentials within the brain itself. Berger, the originator of electroencephalography, was himself interested in the EEG as possibly revealing an initial source of energy that is somehow transformed into what he called a "psychic energy." He thought this "psychic energy" was responsible for telepathy. But the study of psi has moved ahead since Berger's time and we no longer look for an energetic source of transmission of ESP. Berger, however, may still be proven a prophet in his search for a connection between psi and the EEG, for research in this area, too, has progressed a bit since his time.

Berger discovered within the brain certain relatively large 10-cycle-per-second rhythms which are usually called alpha rhythms. It now appears that Berger's 10-cycle waves may be related to ESP scoring. But before discussing the possible relation of ESP and alpha waves, let us see what the alpha rhythms mean in terms of the behavior and psychology of the normal person. When a person is relaxed, yet not drowsing, and has his eyes closed, the 10-cycle-per-second alpha rhythm is present. If the person opens his eyes or tries to visualize something, the rhythm disappears. The rhythm will also be disrupted by any startling stimulus. Additionally, the alpha rhythm can be observed if a person is placed in a dark room and he is not visualizing or trying to "see his way in the dark." In general, then, the presence of the 10-per-second alpha rhythm is associated with a relaxed condition of mind which is devoid of disturbance from outside sources or attempts at visualization. If, however, the relaxation turns into drowsiness the alpha rhythm gives way in this case as well.

From this knowledge about alpha rhythms, it is a short step to a hypothesis about the possible relationship of alpha and ESP. Many persons who have tested ESP experimentally would probably agree that a relaxed frame of mind, yet one fixed upon the task and devoid of any drowsiness, is often conducive to good scoring, especially if the proper motivation is present. We might expect, therefore, a greater abundance of alpha rhythms when the subject is doing well on the ESP test, provided of course that one factor associated with his doing well is his relaxed frame of mind.

Cadoret and Fahler, working at the Duke Parapsychology Laboratory in 1957-58, brought to light in an unpublished exploratory study some data which tend to confirm the alpha-ESP hypothesis just mentioned. They were able to predict with a significant degree of success whether a given ESP run was high- or low-scoring on the basis of the relative amount of alpha shown in the subject's brain rhythms. The relative amount of alpha required differed for different individuals, but the basic relationship between higher scores and greater alpha appeared quite consistent.

Currently I am engaged at the Parapsychology Laboratory in an attempt to see if the general results of Cadoret and Fahler can be duplicated. This project, as now under way, incorporates several modifications of the original Cadoret-Fahler experiment. The basic emphasis has been to simplify the design of the earlier work.

In the current experiment, like the original, the subject guesses the identity of a shuffled deck of ESP cards enclosed in a box which is lying on a table. In the Cadoret-Fahler work, however, the subject was first hypnotized and given suggestions to help put him at ease. It was hoped this would allow the subject to show some ESP in the test situation, since he would be relieved of any tensions or misgivings he might feel about being subjected to the scalp electrodes and the almost medical atmosphere of the surroundings. In the present work, it is felt that it should be possible to eliminate the time-consuming, tedious task of hypnotizing subjects prior to the experiment and at the same time to induce by proper procedure a certain relaxation and confidence on the part of the subject. The experimental situation is as informal as possible, and every effort is made to put the subject at ease in the test situation. Nor is the subject enclosed for the test in a wire cage as he was in the former experiment. This cage was used by Cadoret and Fahler for shielding the subject electrically so that the EEG could be properly recorded, but advances in electrode attachment and electronic equipment have made this cage unnecessary in the present experiment.

This modified procedure has paid off well, both in time saved and ESP produced. Hypnosis has been shown to be unnecessary for the production of ESP while recording with the EEG. In the current work at the time of this writing, 123 runs through the ESP deck have been made, using 25 subjects for at least three runs each. The results are good enough to show that ESP is almost certainly occurring, for results with the level of scoring obtained would occur by accident only two or three times out of one thousand such experiments. Thus ESP seems to function quite well under the modified set of conditions.

It is felt that several advances—some mentioned here, others not mentioned—have been made over the earlier procedure. To date, the results look fairly promising for the alpha rhythm hypothesis or some modification of this, but it is too early for any definite conclusions. The present experiment appears to be opening up some new research problems and new approaches and, as such, it is already successful to some degree, since these are important functions in any research area.

I have been asked to report to you on this research in progress, and I have tried to give you a general picture of the work as it stands at present. The EEG is shown as a promising tool, and the problems which such research both answers and poses are too important to be ignored. We have long looked for ways of tracking down the more subtle manifestations of ESP in the individual for ways of capturing those fleeting, here-then-gone-now functions of psi which so cunningly elude the paper-and-pencil questionnaire. Perhaps the EEG with its shuttling, rapidly shifting patterns will be hasty enough to ensnare the phantom psi at work.

13

Some Relations of ESP Scores to Changes in Skin Resistance

by MR. SOJI OTANI

As early as 1934, Dr. J. B. Rhine, in his first monograph, *Extra-Sensory Perception,* pointed out the need to study the physiological aspects of ESP. But even today we have no conclusive data about the relationship between the physiological changes in the subject and his ESP performance. I have found this area of investigation fascinating but difficult.

At the suggestion of Dr. Rhine and because of my own keen interest in the physiological investigation of ESP, I have conducted experiments during the past ten months to look for a possible relationship between ESP scores and the resistance of skin to the passage of electrical current. This afternoon I would like to present to you briefly some aspects of my work. Let me hasten to point out, however, that this is a phase of research in progress rather than a report of work completed.

In studies in general psychology, resistance of the skin to electrical current is used as an index of the level of a person's activation. Change in skin resistance has a close relationship to the activity of the sweat glands, which are controlled by the sympathetic nervous system. When a person is alert, the resistance of his skin to electrical current is low, and when he is relaxed it is relatively high. Consequently, by measuring changes in skin resistance we can get information about whether a person is excited or relaxed. I have tried in my experiments to find out whether the subject's ESP scoring is related to his level of activation as measured by the electrical skin resistance.

The procedure of the experiment was briefly this: A very weak electric current was applied through two electrodes attached to the subject's fingers. The amount of resistance on that part of the subject's skin was determined by measuring the difference in the electrical potential between the electrodes. The state of the subject's skin resistance was recorded continuously by a standard polygraph machine on graph paper moving at a constant speed. This measurement was taken during the entire period of ESP testing and identifying marks were made on the recording paper at the points where the test started and ended. The amount of change in skin resistance was measured by comparing the amount of resistance at the beginning of each session and at the end. In most cases skin resistance increased during the ESP test, although it sometimes decreased.

Each experimental period consisted of 10 or more different periods of measurement. In one experiment a test run of 25 trials and, in another, a time period of one minute was used as a unit for measuring the change in skin resistance. Since each subject was measured 10 or more times during each experimental period, the average value of change in skin resistance for that person was calculated for the period. This measure was used to determine whether the change in skin resistance during each of the measuring units in that experimental period was above or below the average for that series as a whole. Since change in skin resistance was used as a relative index of the degree of the subject's activation during the test, we may call the state in which skin resistance was larger than the average amount "the relaxed condition" and the opposite state, "the excited condition." I recognize, however, that these are not completely accurate expressions.

The results of my earlier experiments indicated that positive ESP scoring is likely to occur when the subject is in a relaxed condition and that negative results may be obtained when he is in an excited condition. In seven out of nine experiments in which I myself was the subject, this tendency was observed.

This result is consistent with what we already know about the mental states conducive to the manifestation of ESP. To obtain positive deviations, the experimenter usually tries to provide an informal atmosphere and to relax the subject and put him at ease before the test.

In two experiments, this tendency to score positively in the relaxed state was reversed. In one of the two (my first experiment conducted here in the Parapsychology Laboratory with myself as the subject), I obtained a significantly positive deviation in the runs made in the excited condition. This puzzling reversal of what seemed to be a common tendency presented a new problem which needed to be tackled before any conclusions could be reached about the relationship between changes in skin resistance and the subject's ESP performance.

When I looked into one of the two experiments in which this reversal had occurred, it became apparent that in spite of the overall tendency in this experiment to obtain more hits in the excited state than in the relaxed, there were, in fact, more hits in the relaxed condition during the first part of the testing. I divided my record sheets, consisting of 20 runs each, into five equal parts in the order in which the subject had done the runs. Then I plotted on a graph the deviations from mean chance expectation for each of these parts for the relaxed and excited conditions separately. As may be seen in Figure 1, there was a small difference in ESP scoring at

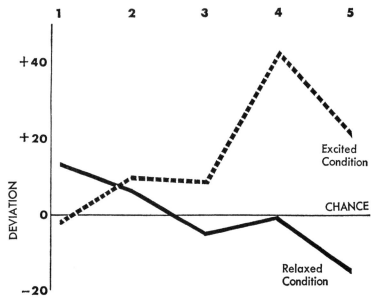

FIG. 1. Distribution of hits for the five sections of the page in the excited and relaxed states.

the beginning which was associated with higher scores for the relaxed condition. As the test progressed, however, the tendency reversed and the difference gradually built up in favor of higher scoring on the excited condition. It can be seen also that the large part of the positive deviation on ESP scores in the excited condition is to be found during the last two sections of the page. While the scores in the relaxed condition gradually fell, the scores in the excited condition rose.

When I analyzed the results of another experiment, I found that it gave a positive deviation only in the relaxed condition and that the position effects showed the same tendency to have the higher scores in the excited condition toward the end of the run. I plotted, on the graph shown in Figure 2, the hit distribution in the five segments of the run for the relaxed and excited conditions separately. As may be seen, the scores in the excited condition began well below the mean in the first segment and gradually rose to above the

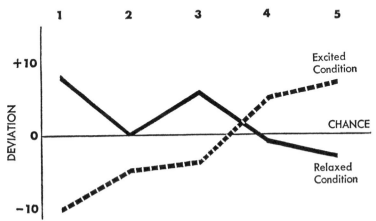

FIG. 2. Distribution of hits for the five segments of the run in the excited and relaxed states.

chance mean during the last segment, whereas the scores in the relaxed condition began above the chance mean in the first segment and gradually fell below the mean during the last segment.

Even though the method of evaluating the position effects in these two experiments is somewhat different because the two tests were conducted differently, there seems to be a meaningful relationship in the way the subject's scores declined in the relaxed condition and inclined in the excited condition. For this reason, it becomes necessary in considering the relationship between skin resistance and ESP scores to take account of the shift of the subject's scoring as the test progresses.

I am not now at a stage where I can draw any reliable conclusions about the relationship between ESP and skin resistance. I do not yet have enough data to do this; but my data, it seems to me, have enough suggestive leads to render the continuation of this aspect of ESP research necessary. The problem indeed is complex and the solution will not be easy. The time of day, the physiological type of the subject, and the nature of the test in which the subject is engaged seem to be important variables with which I would like to deal in my future experiments.

14

Closing Remarks

by DR. K. RAMAKRISHNA RAO

We have now had a look over the shoulders, as it were, of a research team at work in a parapsychology laboratory. The projects that were presented to us do not represent all aspects of the work of these investigators, nor do they constitute the entire group in training.

These men and women are the members of the growing family of the FRNM, and their work represents the expanding frontiers of parapsychological research. It is, therefore, reasonable to hope that the FRNM will play an important role in its support of our quest to conquer the highest peaks of the human mind. The prospects for a growing science of parapsychology and a fuller understanding of man are immensely better for the promise these young workers afford us for the future.

Part III

Parapsychology Today

15

The Status and Prospect of Parapsychology Today

by DR. J. B. RHINE

The four papers of the morning program reviewed the development of parapsychology at Duke. As stated in the introduction, this review was offered as a background and basis for judgment of what may fairly be expected from the extended plans which are being laid with much earnest concern at this time. The afternoon series of short papers by a group of young workers afforded sampling glimpses of researches in actual progress at the moment.

This longitudinal approach to the establishment of the Foundation for Research on the Nature of Man is not, however, the only perspective needed in making this appraisal. That is why *this* hour marks a turning point in the character of today's program, since now another angle of approach will be taken. The emphasis of this paper will be on parapsychology *today,* and upon that science not only as represented at the Duke Laboratory but also wherever research in the field is going on.

This turn is important, however great the inheritance of

standards, traditions, and potential capabilities from the developments at Duke. It is not enough that there is now a healthy growth in this branch of inquiry; that it has made its way through a very trying period; that it now has a substantial scientific literature, a devoted even though small personnel, a growing number of research centers in different parts of the world, few as they are, and an intelligent public interest in its activities.

All this is indeed greatly to be appreciated; but it is rather the recognition of the critical *need* for the Foundation *today,* even more than its heritage, that will determine its continued growth and support. For that reason the leading question back of the present survey will be How much and in what ways does parapsychology today really need this new organization?

At the same time, in turning our backs at this point upon the story of parapsychology at Duke, there is no real break with the past; for the Foundation, in its goal of serving parapsychology with the broadest possible coverage, is only aiming to do more effectively and extensively the task which for many years the Duke Laboratory itself, to the extent of its limited capacities, has undertaken. Accordingly, the transverse view now presented will involve, for the most part, the world-wide network of relations that has grown up between the Duke center and research workers on all the inhabited continents.

For that matter, there is not even an implication of a break in the continuity of the parapsychology program itself as it is moving through its present transfer from the Duke Laboratory to the Foundation's Institute for Parapsychology. This transitional operation is one of steady, unbroken progress for parapsychology in research, in funds, and in the educational program.

I will turn now to an appraisal of the status of parapsychology today in its larger outlines, its strength and its weaknesses, its progress and its needs, its promise and its uncertainties. A candid appraisal, with balanced attention to advantages and difficulties, is required.

* * * * * *

The most impressive fact about parapsychology today is the really enormous amount of public interest in the field. The growth of this interest year after year over several decades is remarkable.

The public attention given to the subject after the first publications from the Duke Laboratory was at first of a generally superficial nature. Over the years, however, this interest has increasingly extended into professional and technological circles and parapsychology has found a place, albeit a modest one, in many textbooks, encyclopedias, and reference works. An extensive scientific literature about psi phenomena has developed, and it is slowly penetrating into the educational system both in the secondary schools and in the colleges.

Such interest is, of course, not confined to this country; in fact, the geographic spread is even more significant. Popular articles and correspondence bring evidence of general attention around the world to what is taking place in parapsychology, and there are indications that it extends also into the universities of other countries. It is no longer, as once was the case, mainly the North Atlantic community of nations that constitutes the area of active interest in this branch of science. Parapsychology has been a research topic for the Ph.D. thesis in a number of different countries, some as far away as Australia and South Africa; and there are professors of parapsychology in Argentina and Chile. New research centers have been established or are being planned in South America, Eastern Europe, and the Far East. The research methods reviewed during the morning program have now been described in many of the world's languages, with new translations continuing into Japanese, Israeli, and Czech, as well as Spanish and German.

Such general interest is, of course, not a static matter. Quite naturally it has depended upon the researches done and the educational effort that made the findings known. But much has depended, too, upon the efforts made at the Duke Laboratory to keep up exchanges with workers in different countries, some of whom have been relatively isolated. It has been possible to supply reading matter to individuals who had little access to adequate libraries, to give advice about research methods, and to aid in some of the many other needs for exchange which the student and research worker experiences. The Visiting Research Fellowship Program which has been maintained in recent years by the Duke Laboratory has aided a number of workers, though all too few, to make visits for research discussions and training. A student's information service has likewise grown up at the Laboratory to supply information to the thousands of high-school students and college undergraduates who annually request it.

Even the counseling of other inquirers—such as editors, publishers, writers, and producers—who deal now and then with matters involving parapsychology has become a service of some magnitude. In this, as in all the other relations directly or indirectly in touch with public interest, there has not been the decline that in earlier years had been anticipated. Public interest in parapsychology seems to be a steady development in itself rather than a passing flurry or fad.

If this is a fair judgment, the growth of this interest is not only of importance to our field, but it represents a responsibility as well. Until the universities arrive at the stage where they can furnish expert leadership and counsel, there needs to be a central organization to which all who need information, counsel, or training may turn for reliable guidance and assistance on the entire range of research and educational services. Such an institution needs to be strong enough to remain independent and objective. This is especially true since interest in parapsychology stems from many related but divergent beliefs and practices.

This developing public interest in psi phenomena has even created some serious problems that the individual worker in the field can hardly be expected to handle alone. It has, for example, made rather profitable certain deceptive practices that are represented as being based on "psychic" powers possessed by the practitioner. Clever and unscrupulous performers are able to take advantage of the public with a greater degree of success because of widespread public knowledge of university researches on ESP and related abilities. This knowledge naturally creates a certain amount of unguarded receptivity. Still other individuals have been able to set themselves up as professional "parapsychologists" without any valid credentials under the shelter of the public confidence in the reliable experimental work that has begun to grow up.

The need for an authoritative clearing house is becoming more obvious as time goes on. At such a qualified center standards of judgment can be set up, methods for testing claims can be taught, and qualifying examinations offered. If this central institution is well planned and supported, it can take leadership also in corrective action against fraudulent practices and can introduce protective (perhaps even legislative) measures against the charlatanism of related areas. In this way the public interest that has been so important for the development of parapsychology could derive benefit and protection. Here, indeed, is an important role for the Foundation to play.

* * * * * *

For the second general impression of parapsychology today I choose, for balance, one that is much less gratifying; namely, that the research is moving very slowly. Not only is it lagging behind normal expectation in acceptance by the other sciences, but the research itself must appear to an impartial observer as advancing at a disappointing rate in comparison with most other fields of science. The number of papers published annually is not showing the increase to be expected from a thriving new branch of inquiry. Twenty-seven years after the founding of the *Journal of Parapsychology* there is still no reserve backlog of papers awaiting publication. And the *Journal* is still a quarterly. This is a sobering fact.

The picture is somewhat altered, however, by taking into account how few people are doing research in parapsychology on a full-time basis. Modest as the opportunities have been at the Duke Laboratory, with an average team of four to five full-time workers on the doctoral level, there has been nothing even comparable to it in opportunity anywhere else in the world. In fact, most of the research contributors to parapsychology have been operating on a part-time basis; and in all fairness it must be said that even at the Duke Laboratory, with all the additional duties that fall upon the individual, the theoretically full-time worker does well to average half time on his own research.

Add to this situation the fact that there has been an unusually large turnover of staff members (as is to be expected in a young branch of inquiry for which there exists no graduate department for training and selection of personnel). The candidate who would normally spend four or five years getting ready to work in any other field merely starts to work in parapsychology when he becomes sufficiently interested; he then finds out through years of experience whether or not he is in the right field. (Incidentally, the laboratory to which he becomes attached simply has to absorb the risks and the wear and tear of this frontier way of acquiring permanent personnel.) What wonder if not many are able to qualify and become professional parapsychologists?

But even with all the present facility of entry into this field, there are still only a small number of active research workers on the job in parapsychology today, and the number is not showing a proper and healthy increase. There have, in fact, been at least a few unfilled vacancies and opportunities for trained and experienced personnel for several years.

These candid clues will serve to introduce the underlying reason for the slow research progress in parapsychology. There simply are too few qualified people taking part. It has been evident for some time in America and Western Europe that interested young scientists are hesitant to enter this field of research. Some admit they fear the effect that choosing parapsychology, even as an avocation, would have upon their professional status. They recognize that the prospect for their advancement would likely be affected by an open participation in the field. It can be supposed, too, that they are all naturally sensitive to what their colleagues would think; it is entirely normal to be so.

This pressure is felt not merely at the end point of decision; it is exerted throughout the educational program of the individual. The interest of the large numbers of high-school students who, year after year, do science fair projects or other special studies on parapsychology dwindles through the college years, and with only a very few does an active interest in psi survive the graduate and professional schools. Quite understandably the student drifts away from the subject when he finds little or no attention being paid to it by his teachers, or when he encounters misleading or unfavorable impressions in the course of his class discussions.

It is the plan of the Foundation, however, to change this situation. The program of the Stone Fund for Parapsychological Education, which was announced today, represents a point of departure in this new direction. It means that the time has come for parapsychology to take a degree of educational initiative.

The bright, courageous students who turn each year to look hopefully at the promise of this new field deserve to be armed with literature adequate to prepare them for the possible depreciative comments on parapsychology which are offered now and then by an ill-informed instructor. Effective encouragement can be given to the formation on college campuses of student groups to foster study, discussion, and introductory research on psi problems. With suitable literature and other educational material, and with scholarship aid much more freely provided, the Foundation expects to develop throughout the educational world a more accurate impression of psi research. There is no need to leave uncorrected the very grave misunderstanding of the case for parapsychology that is passed along from one class to another on many school campuses.

It is, of course, time for vigorous steps to be taken to make parapsychology a professional field which the young scientist will be both pleased to join and safe in entering—if he is qualified. The setting-up of a strongly staffed Institute under the Foundation will encourage and aid other centers to get started. These new positions will have to be well provided for and reasonably secure. In the past, parapsychologists have seldom had normal assurance of tenure in their positions.

These new full-time professional research jobs will also encourage part-time work in university positions, especially if more can be done to assist such research with grants in aid. Many college campuses are already open to project research by students if assistance and guidance are assured.

Perhaps the most beneficent influence the Foundation can exert upon the minds of those who are interested in doing something in psi research will derive from the simple fact that such an institution is a reality—that it does exist! Its assets will serve an added purpose: to give assurance. Thus the Foundation's strength is parapsychology's security; and it will serve as an establishment with which to identify. The very existence of a sustaining organization after the decades of controversy and uncertainty is a monument to the successful outcome of the contest. Its mere presence—if we can make it a genuinely sturdy institution—will be all the encouragement the rightfully cautious candidate needs. Then, for the first time, the proper selection of research personnel will become possible.

* * * * * *

The third main impression of the field of parapsychology today to which I would draw attention is the one that gives to this field most of its present strength. It is the impression that the research findings of this field are now definitely and increasingly "making sense." They fit together in a highly satisfactory way and show the lawful order one expects to find in a branch of natural science. This is especially important because it is from these evidences of internal consistency that the logical structuring of a science is composed. It is through the similarity of these orderly patterns to the rest of what we know about nature that the new branch becomes acceptable, first to the workers themselves and then, by way of their reports, to all who eventually come to know and appreciate the findings.

It is always the case in any field that rational acceptance takes place as soon as, but only when, the new parts become structured in a meaningful way. The findings reviewed this morning, which made possible a systematic, unified view of the field as a whole (so that parapsychology could be considered a science) were a major contribution to this stage of "making sense"; and the progress, of course, will continue. But other contributions coming from other workers have been built into this developing rationale, and this larger synthesis, also, still goes on.

How much sense does parapsychology seem to be making today? First of all, the very fact that psi phenomena can be investigated by the same basic approach used throughout the whole of natural science is a truly major point. Like all science, it began with strange observations which people could not explain. Out of the collection of such experiences there grew certain types of happenings for which names were later coined, such as clairvoyance, telepathy, precognition. Then, from these classified experiences came the suggestion that perhaps some mysterious powers of the mind might be causing these effects. The basic approach of testing such trial ideas, which is essential to all science, was then applied. Early experimental tests were encouraging and led to better ones, and these confirmed the original experiences. Eventually the experimenters, improving their techniques as they went, continued on to isolate and test one type of ability after another, and they found that each one could be experimentally confirmed—telepathy, clairvoyance, precognition, and psychokinesis. In fact, the very properties of lawful order in nature that permitted science to develop in various other fields were holding in this new branch, too; otherwise there would have been no such beginnings. Also, the same mathematics was used, the same experimental principles, the same logic of design and interpretation. Results thus obtained would obviously have to make sense to those who knew about them. It is the way of all science!

Then, as the research advanced, it began to be evident that certain conditions connected with one kind of phenomenon applied also to the others. Clairvoyance appeared in dreams; but dreams bring messages of telepathic nature, too, and of precognition. As other special forms of experience—for example, intuition—were found to be the bearers of parapsychical communications, the various types and forms of psi seemed to hang together too well to be fundamentally independent. General properties, also, seemed to apply to all four types: telepathy, clairvoyance, precognition, and psychokinesis. One such property could be observed to be that of unconciousness, so that the subject in taking a test could not describe how he succeeded when his scores were high or why he failed when he obtained only chance results.

Exactly the same obscurity of consciousness applied to all the types and led to the generalization that psi as a whole is an unconscious process.

And yet it was clear that the subject could aim his ability at a certain target; and, if he succeeded in hitting it, he showed that the capacity was voluntary and, to a certain extent, dirigible, even though it was unconscious. He could direct the ability to some extent to the right object at the right place and time. And, again, this quality of purposive direction was general for all psi effects.

Going from one point to another as scientific studies continued, it was seen that the four types of psi phenomena appeared to be manifestations of a basic underlying unitary function. Psi became one instead of four, although it still has four phenomenological branches. It is just this kind of rational structuring of verified findings into a unified system that constitutes a science. No one can study the progress of this construction of an orderly system from the fragmentary findings of this field without appreciating that this step-by-step construction of a body of knowledge from its experimentally tested parts represents the very real rational strength of parapsychology today.

But even the difficulties of psi research—and they are outstanding ones—reveal an orderly generality and to a certain extent make sense. Take first the unconsciousness of psi and the effect this has on its control. As previously stated, this character applies to all the types and forms of psi phenomena. Psi-missing, or the unconscious avoidance of the target, is equally troublesome in all. So too are all the other uncertainties that are due to the unconscious level on which the ability functions, such as declines in scoring, the unaccountable loss of ability, and the curious displacement effect (that is, the consistent hitting of the target adjacent to the correct one). All are as likely to occur in a test of one type of psi as they are in another. All are equally subject to the variations of unconscious eccentricities in the subject's mind. It is something indeed to know that these handicaps are lawful; this fact is at least an implied promise of eventual solution. And these odd effects of unconsciousness help us to see *why* psi is so elusive a phenomenon and *how* subjects can so easily lose their way and systematically avoid the target while trying to hit it.

The other leading source of mystery about psi is one that, to a degree, also makes sense. I refer to the almost complete lack of information still obtaining of what it is that energizes psi phenomena. It was pointed out in one of the forenoon papers that all types of psi phenomena showed the same nonphysical character in their lack of any general and reliable relation to physical test conditions. This is to say, of course, that the energy which we must suppose is doing the work has to be a nonphysical energy.

But the lawfulness of this mystery of the nature of psi involves more than its consistency among all the kinds of psi phenomena. It is even distinctive enough to serve as a boundary line for parapsychology, enabling us to define parapsychology as the science of the nonphysical functions in personal agency or behavior. Again, this nonphysical character of psi affords the best basis for comparison with the sensorimotor system. It has been pointed out from time to time that nothing like the sensory receptors and motor effectors have been in any way indicated in connection with psi phenomena. No ports of entry like the sense organs and no instrument of energy communication like the muscles have even been looked for. Why should they be expected? The sense organs are, after all, organic meters evolved to intercept physical action, and the conditions under which psi operates rule out physical action as a basis of communication.

As a matter of fact, psi fits into the system of personality reasonably well as far as the facts are known. The contrast of psi with *general* psychology seems to be confined to the sensorimotor system. Otherwise psi seems to function as a normal, healthy ability, responsive to motivational drives, and as part of the general unconscious system of the individual. It is, after all, only in the sensorimotor branch that the energetic basis of personal action is even partially understood in general psychology. But the basic nature of the rest of the human personality is, like the nature of psi itself, a mystery; and one can at least suspect that these two mysteries are closely related.

Thus it can be said, in summary, that since we now know that psi communication is a real process in nature, it provides in its very unifying interaction between subject and object another bridge-work of relations besides the sensorimotor exchange, one that the rational mind can follow as it traces nature's pathways. There is no stopping point, no place for science to draw the line and say this should not or cannot be further explored. Our aim in the understanding of man as a person is to get nature's story in full in much the same way that the earlier sciences have succeeded in doing in their specific domains. It makes good sense to keep right on into the remaining mystery of our species, which is the least understood of them all. Within the proper framework of science there are no stopping points. Science adapts its methods to the problem and just keeps on.

A major difficulty does arise, however, in the clash between the rationale of psi and the existing scientific culture of our time. This blockage could be fatal—it has already been very obstructive—to the progress of the research in parapsychology. At this point, too, the individual research worker, as a rule, is helpless. It is this great task of bridging the gap between the firmly established results of decades of parapsychological research and the existing professional groups of scientists to whom these findings should have significance that the Foundation must regard as perhaps a prior responsibility. This section of the advancement of our science has become the limiting one, the bottleneck.

Fortunately it is evident that as the scientific mind becomes acquainted with the full rationale of the work of parapsychology, its misapprehensions are dissipated and its resistance is lowered. But the ordinary methods of education, the publication of papers, books, and such, are ineffectual with minds that are partially closed by misunderstandings and by the too-ready acceptance of antagonistic philosophical assumptions. Only a patiently directed program of careful presentation of the sense that parapsychology does make can be expected to reach those few who are needed to turn the tide and lead the others to a sensible look at the long-rejected findings. This clearance comes first as a Foundation responsibility because it will open the academic channels of classroom and laboratory to the free flow of the new knowledge of psi to the future workers in parapsychology.

This larger educational task of the Foundation calls for careful staff planning. It will require preparatory study of the present clash of new fact with old theory and of reformulation of findings for readier comprehension. The results that make sense for the parapsychologist may only need translation to another "language" to become reasonable, also, to a whole profession of scientists. All facts, it must be assumed, will eventually become rationally acceptable; and the timing of this can surely be shortened by simple clarification. To do it is, however, a considerable undertaking.

*   *   *   *   *   *

One of the less felicitous impressions one gets of parapsychology today is that it is a much more difficult field than it used to be. In fact, it is gradually dawning upon us all that in the very nature of its research problems it is a very much harder branch of science.

This judgment is made without overlooking the fact that workers in this field are under many handicaps that neighboring sciences do not have to the same extent: limitations of funds, lack of well-staffed and well-equipped centers, and a want of encouraging interest from neighboring disciplines. The difficulties could not be accounted for by the absence of such advantages, however. They would not be overcome entirely, at least not immediately, by the sudden provision of all the many facilitating conditions that are needed. Psi research would still be extraordinarily difficult.

One sees many indications of this relative difficulty. A considerable number of those workers long identified with parapsychology have definitely recognized their inability to elicit evidence of psi in the experimental test situations normally used. There are, of course, many useful things for a worker to do besides actively participating as an experimental tester.

Moreover, some of those who have succeeded to a degree have had long searches for one or, perhaps, two or three individual subjects with whom they were able to get a sufficient manifestation of psi to justify their continuing research. It has been recognized since the late 1930's that the psychological conditions under which testing is done are highly important and that the interpersonal relations between subject and experimenter largely determine the results. Accordingly, these experimenters who have had little or no success with subjects and those who have succeeded only with a limited few help to draw further attention to the extreme difficulty of the field at what might be called the shoreline, the very beginning of the collecting of evidence.

Another of the more general signs of the difficulty of this field can be appreciated by those who have kept in view the occasional effort, over the years, of a venturesome general psychologist here and there who decides to design and conduct an experiment in parapsychology without benefit of counsel from someone experienced in catching the elusive psi. Over the last three decades a considerable number of such attempts have been made on both sides of the Atlantic, most probably many more times than have been reported. In most of these experiments there has been a reasonably competent "arm-chair" design, suitable for a general psychology project. The work is planned on the assumption that if ESP is a genuine ability, it ought to be counted on to show itself in much the same way as memory or learning or subliminal vision. None of these experiments have ever, to my knowledge, produced appreciable evidence of psi. In some instances these experiments are reported as having been carried out in "the correct way," as if to imply that something must be wrong with the other experiments that have yielded positive results. Actually the time and effort spent on these misguided excursions have been wasted.

What these many ill-conceived experiments do indicate is that psi cannot be dealt with in the absence of a research worker capable of producing it—that is, able to obtain results under adequately controlled conditions. Recognition of this basic natural requirement has been slow, although it was emphasized in 1937 in the first handbook from the Duke Laboratory. As a matter of fact, although this is a psychological difficulty, it has been hard to make clear even to the psychologists themselves. One may well wonder, therefore, if the engineer or physicist or chemist who comes into parapsychology may be ready to appreciate at once the subtle psychological relations required between experimenter and subject in an adequate test. It is, in fact, rare that the newcomer from any background can at once sufficiently appreciate the difficulty confronting him.

The impression that parapsychology is even more difficult now than formerly comes partly from the fact that the researches of today are reaching out farther into related areas. Some of them definitely call for special training or for collaboration with specialists in the areas concerned. This was conspicuous, for example, in the work on psi in animals. It is equally true of the physiological studies now going on; it is involved in current problems touching upon medical research, and other such border areas as well.

But perhaps the greatest difficulty parapsychology offers to test the researcher's capability is in the demand it makes upon his entire scientific orientation. Probably no field was ever approached by inquirers who were dominated by such a great variety of assumptions, backgrounds, philosophies, and special interests. One inquirer, for example, is interested only in verifying his belief that direct mental action can heal organic disease. Another is as specifically concerned with demonstrating dowsing as a manifestation of unknown physical forces. A third is interested very simply in knowing whether psi can be applied reliably to communication with discarnate personal agencies. Still another is a dedicated anti-materialist who wants materialism disproved scientifically. Some are after new methods of communicating in outer space. The list, if complete, would be a long one.

These special interests may be worthy in themselves, but they can easily become handicaps to those who want to be parapsychologists on the level of methodological standards that have made the field what it is. The viewpoint of the individual's general approach may be too limiting for a good objective research program, or the standards of the field may not permit a sufficiently rapid or direct attack upon the special interest of that particular worker. The adjustments required in order to make a worker most effective in the search for the truth which parapsychology can offer tend to pull him away from any overemphasis relating to his former field of specialization and to make him, rather, a humble searcher for whatever the truth of nature really is. This is a difficult adjustment for those who have a cherished theory or a warmly espoused belief, as a large proportion of those who come into the field do have.

But although parapsychology is a harder field of research

today than formerly and is becoming more so, nevertheless more ambitious programs of inquiry are penetrating the boundaries of the neighboring disciplines. It also offers greater opportunity and greater challenge just because of all the difficulties I have been listing. If not everyone who may wish to be is able to be a parapsychologist, then on this point, too, our field is just like every other.

Even if the special requirements are more difficult than those of many other fields—and I think they are—this only accents the importance of the better selection of personnel and of having an agency to assume some responsibility in such matters. The Foundation's education program already referred to is aimed not only toward more help and encouragement for those coming on but, at the same time, toward more of an opportunity for them to find out how well they can do in research of this nature before getting too deeply committed. It is more than just a matter of finding a greater number of capable workers. A glance over the history of the personnel of the field shows that there is a tendency for the frustrated experimenter—one whose efforts give him only chance results—to turn into an embittered and implacable denigrator of the whole field. Such persons should be screened earlier and directed to fields more suited to their gifts and dispositions.

The Institute for Parapsychology will be staffed and extended to provide a training ground and, incidentally, a self-testing ground for those who need the opportunity to discover their own potential. It will furnish conditions that favor the individual in developing his experimental gifts. It is most probable that many of those who have failed in their own unaided efforts to get evidence of ESP could have been saved this failure by preparatory training.

The program that is aimed at so difficult a field needs more than trained, well-selected workers. The Institute must be prepared for the kind of teamwork that calls for specialists in whatever disciplines can best contribute. And yet we must not attempt to elevate the prestige of the Institute by the mere variety of professions represented, nor even by their distinction. It is one of the first objectives of the Foundation's program to help the world to appreciate parapsychology itself as a legitimate and respectable profession with its own unique problems and difficulties. Then, and only then, will the scholar crossing over from another field recognize his need of special preparation. He must not be allowed to think that merely stepping across an imaginary line will make him, in some miraculous way, as much of a parapsychologist as, let us say, he was a physicist or general psychologist or physiologist. The specific transfer value from one field to another in parapsychology has not proved thus far to be very great in any case.

Obviously the laboratory that can accomplish all these needed objectives will have to be built and developed. *If* it cannot make parapsychology easier in terms of making its problems smaller, simpler, less ambitious, or narrower, it can help to make it a field occupied by workers increasingly well trained for their research tasks and better selected for the peculiar needs of this field. Above all, it should help to prepare the parapsychologist for an appreciation of the magnitude of the service his field can render to the understanding of man and for a valuation of that field on its *own* independent terms. This intellectual independence, the highest freedom of the human mind, is a most precious requirement for such a foundation as ours. We are dedicated to try to find the men and women able to match and preserve it.

*   *   *   *   *   *

My final major impression of parapsychology today is fortunately a more reassuring one. I have the view, which I think is more than a mere projection of my own optimism, that our science today is taking on a confident mood that is at once wholesome and constructive. Individual judgments differ, of course—in parapsychology perhaps more than in most research groups. But there are signs that are reasonably objective. One of these signs is the relative indifference parapsychologists show to the hostile critic of the field today as compared to the nervous tension that in earlier times resulted from the appearance of a critical attack. Today, not only does the parapsychologist feel the new confidence I mention, but also I can detect a state of resignation on the part of the opposition. For example, repeated attempts have been made in recent years to set up a round-table or symposium in which a critic of parapsychology would present the case against it. It has been difficult to find anyone willing to represent that side, although the time was when such critical representatives were plentiful enough and very willing.

The calmer attitude in parapsychology may be partly due to the acceptance of the fact that it is likely to be a long time before there is a general recognition of parapsychology in the universities and the professions in this country. A certain independence of mind among us is raising the question why this psi research group cannot make an independent profession of its own. The desire for identification with older professional groups is coming to appear as a misplaced emphasis, an underestimation of the actual grounds for the independence of parapsychology. It is, in fact, time for it to be more widely realized that parapsychology does not actually belong to *any* of the sciences as they are today. To say that it is properly a branch of psychology (as we have been doing) is to idealize psychology. There is no field of science that now recognizes, even as a possibility, the kind of reality to which the evidence of parapsychology offers support.

I think today's parapsychologist is saying, "Very well, then. If the territory we have discovered is not wanted in another field, that makes it all the more our own. If we ourselves appreciate its uniqueness and the soundness of our claims, why should we feel inferior in our identification and ownership, and in our plans for the exploitation of it?"

As a result of this attitude, parapsychologists, with all their limitations and difficulties, are acquiring a bit of proper professional pride and the confidence that, from here on, there will always be a parapsychology. Since we know the position of parapsychology is sound, we can well enough and with more equanimity allow time for the fact to be appreciated. The related disciplines will, of course, have to adjust eventually, but the timing is up to them.

If this calmer temper of parapsychology today can now be supported by a strong, independent institution of the kind we are building in this Foundation, I think we may expect very gratifying accomplishments ahead. If now I speak of some of these, it is not to speculate upon them, but rather to indicate what we may do about them right from the starting point.

First of all, if we look upon our field as an independent branch of science which includes an important section of nature in its coverage, *it is this branch of science* which will take the initiative in expanding its relationships and bridge the gaps so that eventually it will be part of the larger scientific picture. We will move out from where *we* are to these inter-connecting linkages. We will command the bridges and take the offensive in the explorations that are needed. It is parapsychology, not general psychology, that will continue to look into those interrelations between these branches that now are so important to the understanding of our own results. In our large common ground with physiology, too, it is parapsychology that will establish the exchange, already beginning, that will integrate the psi researches with the biological order of nature. This initiative is already ours.

In other words, the time has come when we can confidently cease to defend our boundaries and proceed to cross them. Let us, as the best example, leave behind the older issues about the nature of psi with respect to the physical world. In the past, for various reasons it has been important to emphasize that psi does not fit the concept of the physical world. Yet it is not possible to think of psi reasonably without assuming a determining energy. This would mean, whatever the words we use, that we are thinking of a determining influence in the universe, hitherto unknown, by means of which a person interacts with the physical world. Psi requires a nonphysical energy to make sense.

But while we have needed to be concerned in the past with the nonphysicality of psi, it is profitable now to go on from there to the problem of energy exchange or conversion. Certain operations of physical energies themselves are observable and measurable only indirectly through conversion to another energetic state, as is the case with psi. We need to learn how the conversion of energy which makes it possible for psi to be a discoverable part of the universe actually occurs. What is the locus of this conversion, and what are its conditions? What are the properties of psi energy beyond those general characteristics already available from the psi data? It must not be expected that the physicists themselves, looking from their own windows, will ever see this problem as theirs. Very well, it is already ours! And the time has now come when we have the confidence to be properly and openly proud of its magnitude and have the courage to attack it.

There is one more bold step we are taking in this more confident mood of today. It is one that particularly needs the added assurance given by this Foundation. We dare to speak out now about the far-reaching implications of the findings of parapsychology, even as they are today, without waiting for that later stage of fuller understanding, controlled application, and many other reasonably likely developments of the future. The simple fact that psi does occur (under the conditions it does) requires the addition of a whole new distinctive category of nature to provide for it—an extra-physical branch of reality intuitively conceived by men through the ages but never before recognized in the sciences. Some parapsychologists, however, up until now have tactfully avoided stressing this radical nature of their findings, hoping to stir up less opposition. Whatever the wisdom of this bit of diplomacy, the mood of today is becoming more candid. There will be those who still must continue to speak with restraint, whether to meet the requirements of a party line or of an academic line. But there is more urge today than ever before to spell out forthrightly what the facts of parapsychology mean—and to let the chips fall where they may!

It is about time! There has never been a greater need to know what man has within his nature for use in self-understanding and self-regulation. If there is—and we now know there is—some unknown, distinctive, determining causality in man that can be explored by science, this finding must necessarily raise hopeful questions in any intellectually honest and truly free mind that knows and appreciates the fact. But forthright action is fully as essential as the knowledge itself. Let us remember that most of us would not be alive today had medicine, at a similar stage in its history, remained as indifferent to the first claims of the germ theory of disease as the disciplines of today have been to the findings about psi. But the initiative is always with the explorers and their sense of urgency in reaching their goals.

How important is it, then, that we explore further this unknown side of human personality represented by psi? It is reason enough that man's efforts in the past to understand himself, from his religions down to his current anti-religious ideologies, have all played constantly (pro or con) with this thesis of an invisible, immaterial, spiritual, ideal, or psychical part of man. It is time now to push the research on into this hidden part of man's nature with all the best methods that scholarship can offer. If there is any more important area of inquiry than that to submit to science, no one has thought of it yet. The Foundation for Research on the Nature of Man has been hopefully created to lead us all in facing this responsibility as forthrightly as our powers will permit. Using the techniques of inquiry that have already been developed by the parapsychologists of the past, we will endeavor to discover what meaning our findings have for the understanding of man's nature, what more can be added, and what this world beyond the category of physics contains for man's fuller self-understanding and for the enlightenment of his conduct of life.

For a long time it has seemed that parapsychology has just not had headroom enough to allow its leadership to stand up boldly for the findings it has persistently and repeatedly confirmed and especially for their manifest implications. But as I read the indications now, there is a new readiness to make the most of these discoveries for the significance they clearly seem to have for man's life today, whatever discipline they touch upon. And to accommodate this franker, bolder purpose, the design for the Foundation for Research on the Nature of Man will need to be appropriately expansive. Our work, our program, and our vision are notably less constricted than ever they have been before.

The work ahead in parapsychology will continue to have no less careful attention to detail, the same rigorous control, and all the cautious supervision of the past; but the free range of a more confident intellectual atmosphere which will accompany these laboratory developments will give comparable scope for a larger constructive synthesis. For the scientific findings will be fitted by means of every reasonable and possible application to the great questions about the guiding principles of life to which, in the past, men have brought only speculation and intuition. Through this Foundation—representing those who work within it as well as those whose studies have led up to it, and those who contribute to it as much as those who keep it operating—science will be enabled, after all its sweeping conquests of the outer worlds of space and time, of computers and molecules, of galaxies and microparticles, to catch up at last with man himself and help him to discover the side of his own nature, which, for the better guidance of life, he needs so badly to know.

Part IV

Appendix

Appendix A

Program
for

FOUNDATION DAY

Celebrating the Establishment of the

FOUNDATION FOR RESEARCH ON THE NATURE OF MAN

July 30, 1964

Meetings Sponsored by the Parapsychology Laboratory

Duke University

PROGRAM

10:00 a.m. - Noon Social Science Auditorium - Room 139

PARAPSYCHOLOGY AT DUKE IN REVIEW (1927-1965)
Chairman: Dr. J. B. Rhine

Beginnings in the Department of Psychology:
ESP Established
Dr. Winnifred M. Nielsen

Parapsychology Becomes a Branch of Science
Dr. John A. Freeman

The Place of Psi in the Natural Order
Dr. K. Ramakrishna Rao

Advancement Toward Control and Application
Dr. Louisa E. Rhine

12:30 - 1:45 p.m. Luncheon
Old Trinity Room, Union Building, West Campus
Dr. Marie R. Higbee, Presiding
Announcements
Dr. Louisa E. Rhine

2:15 - 3:30 p.m. Social Science Auditorium - Room 139

SOME CURRENT RESEARCHES IN PROGRESS AT DUKE
Chairman: Dr. K. Ramakrishna Rao

An ESP Experiment with Two-language Targets
Miss B. K. Kanthamani

An Exploratory Test of ESP in Relation to Anxiety
Proneness
Mr. James C. Carpenter

The Measurement of PK (Psychokinesis) by Electric
Clocks
Mr. Robert Lyle Morris

Comparisons of Performance in Memory and ESP Tests
Mrs. Sally Rhine Feather

A Study of Relations Between ESP Scoring and "Brain
Waves" (EEG)
Mr. Rex G. Stanford

Some Relations of ESP Scores to Changes in Skin
Resistance
Mr. Soji Otani

4:00 - 5:00 p.m. Open House - Parapsychology Laboratory
West Duke Building, East Campus

6:00 - 8:00 p.m. Dinner
Old Trinity Room
Dr. John Freeman, Presiding

Report of the Secretary
Dr. Marie R. Higbee

A Financing Program for the Foundation
Mr. W. Clement Stone, Chairman

8:30 p.m. Physics Auditorium - Room 114

THE STATUS AND PROSPECT OF PARAPSYCHOLOGY TODAY
Dr. J. B. Rhine

Appendix B

FRNM
BULLETIN

The
Foundation for Research
on the
Nature of Man

Announcement

The Foundation for Research on the Nature of Man is a new institution devoted to advancing the understanding of the human individual. Its attention is directed, not to the broad range of properties man is known to have in common with his physical environment, but, rather, to the scientific discovery of what it is that distinguishes him as a person.

In the past men have had to rely on beliefs too subjective to allow universal agreement and enduring vitality, so that the light afforded for the guidance of human conduct has been a dim and flickering one. Today it is clear that the fullest possible knowledge of man's unique qualities is needed as a basis for the larger measure of self-control to which he aspires and of which he is capable.

In addition to its primary role as a research organization, the Foundation will function as an independent world center for the problem areas it undertakes to cover. It will serve as a headquarters for the clearance of ideas from and the coordination of efforts in many lands and cultures as these focus on the common objective of the understanding of man.

The foundation will help to bridge the gap between the academic community and the isolated researchers, between the sources of support and the needy project, and between an intelligently interested public and the experimental laboratory.

Rationale

The purpose of the Foundation can be stated simply: It will explore fully and carefully all the unusual types of experiences known to man that suggest underlying capacities or principles as yet unrecognized. This search is, of course, the logical one for exploring any new frontier. It is aimed at the discovery of explanatory forces, factors or relations that make a person uniquely what he is. These studies will follow the most reliable ways of ascertaining and verifying knowledge and, at the same time, will be as inclusive as the sensitive skills of scholarship can make them.

In a word, the program is nothing more nor less than a part of the scientific search for whatever lies behind the remaining mysteries of nature, in this case those peculiar to the personality of man. The strange manifestations that remain to challenge the sciences of the mind seem as miraculous as anything in the origins of the recognized branches of science. At least man can lose nothing by the acquisition of all the facts behind these mysteries; certainly he cannot hope to understand himself fully without them.

The Institute

The first research unit established by the Foundation is the Institute for Parapsychology. It deals with man's most puzzling range of experiences, those which clearly seem to transcend the known forces of his physical environment and which best appear to distinguish his specific nature. As a branch of inquiry already far advanced in methods, and with a body of confirmed knowledge well tested by decades of controversy, parapsychology is the subject of study qualified to lead the advance further into the territory of what identifies man.

Background

The Institute for Parapsychology is the designated heir to the Parapsychology Laboratory of Duke University. Already the properties, traditions and standards of the Laboratory are in the process of gradual transfer to the new center. Over the formative years in which it was supported by the University, the Laboratory staff was able to develop methods, train personnel, advance scientific publications and promote worldwide interest in the field. At the same time, the increasing responsibilities of the center have come to require an independent, self-governing and self-sustaining institution, *inter*-university in character, and international in scope. Indeed, in the very utilization of its academic opportunities and advantages parapsychology at Duke has progressively outgrown its link with the university organization which provided them.

Timing

More is involved than the timeliness of this graduation from Duke. Today more than ever a strong, independent organization is needed to help sustain and coordinate far-flung activities in parapsychology. It will probably be many years before an opportunity for graduate training in this research will be provided in university departments in the United States or Western Europe; serious limitations of one kind or another are to be found in other countries as well. But under the guidance of an international center, the contribution of one country may be joined with that of another into a global network of cooperation. If one is taking the lead in methods, another will have a more favorable culture, and a third can provide ingenious apparatus or funds or personnel. Parapsychology needs them all, and each needs the others.

The situation of parapsychology is particularly critical today because of the stage this branch of science has reached. While it has firmly established the *occurrence* of psi phenomena, it still has not reached the second main stage which every new science must attain—that of *control* over its phenomena. Progress toward such control is good, but controlled application for practical use is still like a bridge with an uncompleted span.

Program

The Institute for Parapsychology will extend its coverage as far as its commitments and its facilities permit. Even so, it is not envisioned as equal to the full scope of the Foundation's program. The Foundation for Research on the Nature of Man will, therefore, in due course establish other special institutes within its domain as the need and the prospect of support for them sufficiently develop.

Within the Institute, a program of action on a number of lines is under way. For instance, ownership of the *Journal of Parapsychology* has been acquired. This is probably the most important property in the field. Still another priceless acquisition is the Duke collection of more than 10,000 classified cases of spontaneous psi experience.

Education

A major project of the Foundation is the establishment of the Stone Fund for Parapsychological Education. This provides for aid to a long list of special educational activities. These include scholarship aid, travel grants, assistance in publication and acquisition of books, as well as support of lectures, conferences, symposia and training programs. A five-year project has been established on the initiative of a philanthropic foundation about which a succeeding bulletin will be more explicit.

Connections

The Foundation will be independent but not isolated. It will have functional interchanges with all the institutions with which it cooperates in establishing psi research centers or educational projects. Similarly, there will of necessity be cooperative relations with the centers for which parapsychological workers are being trained. Still other comparable relations on the institutional level may be expected.

Personal connections, too, will be made in a wide variety of ways. These associations extend from membership on the Research Council of the Institute and the Advisory Board of the Foundation to the use many thousands of students make every year of the Student Information Service. To these may be added the many personal ties formed through the Scholarship Fund, the Visiting Research Fellowship Program, the William McDougall Award for Distinguished Work in Parapsychology and the grants in aid for research, training and publication. These interchanges should increase in number and in effectiveness with the growth of the Foundation's capacity to render service.

Location

Growing out of the Duke Laboratory as it did, the Foundation naturally began at Durham. Almost from the founding date, however, questions have been raised many times as to its permanent location. Supporting the already favored proposal that it be at Durham was the gift shortly after the founding of a 50-acre tract of beautifully wooded hills, Chestnut Oak Ridge. The question of location is, however, still open.

Building

Meanwhile, a building committee has been formed and steps have been taken to provide both funds and plans for the first building. Pledges covering more than half the estimated cost have been made, and architectural consultation is being sought. Some major decisions are imminent.

Organization

The founding organization of the Foundation consisted of four members of the Duke Laboratory Staff and their attorney, who made up the Board of Directors. On August 1, 1962, the Board signed a trust agreement establishing the Foundation and appointing the Central Carolina Bank and Trust Company as its Trustee. Tax exempt status was requested of the Internal Revenue Service and has been granted.

Members of the founding Board of Directors pledged themselves to the election of a permanent and enlarged Board in due course. This step has now been taken and the new Board is herein announced.

The schedule of transition from the Duke Laboratory to the Foundation extends to September 1, 1965. A beginning has now been made on the staffing of the Foundation and the Institute for Parapsychology, and this will continue in suitable steps as the present support of the University approaches its scheduled close and the program of relocation makes new demands. The first appointments are announced below.

The appointment of an Advisory Board for the Foundation and of a Research Council for the Institute is, like the selection of the staff, in the "blueprint" stage; but this is, for the present, on schedule. This timing program is needed and good use of it is being made in the basic progress in research, financing and personnel.

Financing

The present support of the Foundation comes principally from gifts of money, securities and real estate by individuals or by philanthropic foundations. Some of it has come through legacies and some by way of trust agreements. Duke has authorized the transfer to the Foundation of certain funds contributed to it for the Parapsychology Laboratory. In November, 1962, a donor who wishes to be anonymous offered to give $1,000,000 within the next five years if $3,500,000 could be raised from other sources.

The most reasonable estimate of the *minimal* support required to do the work expected of the Foundation calls for a total of $5,000,000 in the five-year period ending in December, 1967. Meeting the matching offer would produce $4,500,000. By the time of the final closing of the Duke Laboratory on August 31, 1965, a goal of $1,500,000 should be reached. Funds now on hand, pledged, or otherwise committed sustain confidence that these goals will be met.

The Need

The estimates that have been drawn are modest, but even so a maximum effort will be required to meet them. In order to warrant such an effort a realistic appreciation will be required, not only of what the Foundation can do, but of the world's critical need for this program. The Foundation is being built by more than work and funds and intelligent devotion. Back of it all is a realization of the alarming deficit in man's knowledge of himself. Can we make up this deficit? What will it take? Such unknowns cannot, of course, be closely reckoned. Cost estimates cannot be offered on the understanding of man's nature. But the timing, the rate of progress, the eventual day of fuller self-comprehension, is ours to determine. This much *is* in our hands if these are duly strengthened for the ardors the research demands—in short, if we have the tools to do the job.